"Do we dare Let the Ba[...] [...] [...] [...]itively makes it clear v[...] become the kind of mot[...] ing on the baby for guid[...] act on what we have learned. An important book."
—Marian Tompson, co-founder, La Leche League International

"This is the book Henry David Thoreau would have written if he had been a mother."
—E. Jean Carroll, author, advice columnist, *Elle* magazine

"Lu Hanessian is extraordinarily attuned to her child's needs and her own, in a way that promotes truly wonderful developmental growth. Her book, *Let the Baby Drive*, captures the essence of good parenting with a true blend of Baby Knows Best in tandem with Mother Knows Best. It's a winning combination, reflecting the heart of a child developmental theory, and guarantees raising a happy, healthy child with a solid identity."
—Jane Greer, Ph.D., clinical psycholigist, marital and family therapist, and author of *How Could You Do This to Me? Learning to Trust After Betrayal* and *The Afterlife Connection: A Therapist Reveals How to Communicate with Departed Loved Ones*

"This book is written with the excitement of the first-time mom who stands in awe of the wisdom she received from her baby by listening to him. Lu proves that mothers and babies are a lot smarter than they are usually given credit for being. What a joy to share with other mothers and help them be happier, more fulfilled, stronger to follow their conviction!"
—Tine Thevin, bestselling author of *The Family Bed* and *Mothering and Fathering: The Gender Differences in Child Rearing*

"Finally, the book I have been looking for to recommend to my clients. Lu Hanessian has put into words what I have strived to teach for thirty years. There are many books out there that try to give a 'cookbook' approach to making your children more independent, sleep through the night, be happy and healthy. This book gives you the confidence to find your own approach—your own way with your child."
—Ann Anderson, RN, AAHCC, IBCLC, childbirth/parent educator

Let the Baby Drive

Navigating the Road of New Motherhood

Lu Hanessian

St. Martin's Press ♔ New York

www.stmartins.com

Book design by Gretchen Achilles

Library of Congress Cataloging-in-Publication Data

Hanessian, Lu.
    Let the baby drive / Lu Hanessian.
        p. cm.
    ISBN 0-312-32698-X
    ISBN 13: 978-0-312-32698-2
    1. Child rearing.   2. Motherhood.   I. Title.
    HQ769.H264 2004
    649'.1—dc22   2003026482

First Edition: May 2004

P1

For my one-of-a-kind grandmother Sirvart:

"From nothing, something."

"I could *not* put the book down. I walked around the house with my crying newborn for hours on end, and kept reminding myself of what I had just read. This book made me feel human. I felt such re-assurance. I just didn't want it to end. It resonated with me in a way that no other book on motherhood and parenting has. I'm not a writer, but this book inspired me to want to write. *Let the Baby Drive* has changed the way I think about my child and myself."

ELONA, mother of a newborn and a two-year-old

"*Let the Baby Drive* reads like a comic novel, a private diary, a heart-felt plea, a prayer, and an intimate letter to a friend. There's so much to it. It is that good, that original. Lu Hanessian writes from such an honest core, parts of this book can literally take your breath away."

JANE, mother of a three-year-old

"In this world of experts, everybody has an opinion about how to raise your child—opinions that can get in the way of your relation-ship with your baby. *Let the Baby Drive* clears our path and directs us toward our own children. This book is an enlightenment: it re-minds us that *we* are the experts of our babies. I found this book *so* empowering. It makes us look at our children in a whole new way as we define ourselves as mothers."

"*Let the Baby Drive* resonates with humor, devotion, insight, and honesty. Lu digs into the big questions about identity and understands how parents and children are part of each other's growth. Her unique voice helps us rediscover our *own* intuitive voice, putting parents back in the driver's seat. Finally, a book that's good for *parental* self–esteem!"

"On my journey toward motherhood, I have read many books. *Let the Baby Drive* is a refreshing change, reminding me to be myself and let my child be himself. This book encourages us to listen to our children and learn who they are, instead of molding them into who we think they should be."

"This book is like a giant pat on the back for mothers. Finally, a parenting book that does *not* give advice and yet offers such profound insight into what it means to be a child, a mother, a wife, and a thinking woman. *Let the Baby Drive* made me laugh out loud, cry, think twice, and left me utterly inspired. It's a beautiful book."

CONTENTS

Year One

CHAPTER ONE

Free-falling

e stands on the railing of his crib, one foot on the ledge, the
other swinging back and forth like a Rockette's. It looks like
he's going to fall. I try to lunge forward but can't move a limb.

He is laughing.

I try to scream but can't utter a sound.

I notice he has a mouth full of teeth—in one glimpse, pink gums;
in the next, neat rows of tiny Chiclets gleaming with saliva. He begins
to speak, an adult voice in diapers.

I begin pulling white cotton burp cloths out of his mouth like a
magician tugging scarves from a hat.

His head is covered in spit-up, dipped in it, like cookie batter,
and I'm wiping it with towel after towel, but nothing's coming off.

He's lost. I find him curled up, the size of a sparrow, napping
between two paper plates on a picnic table under a tree.

Seventy-two hours across the threshold of new motherhood,
turbulent hormones bathing my imagination in an intoxicating
brew of euphoria, awe, and mortal terror, these are my dreams.

The sky is black as ink. The dim glow of a nightlight reminds
me of where I am—home—huddled in the rocker with my newborn son in the middle of an icy February. I am holding a gossamer

cloud of a boy, swaddled in pale yellow cotton, his skin soft as flour. A wise old man without wrinkles.

Amnesia sets in. When did I have a baby? When was I ever pregnant? It's as if everything before this birth has faded into snow on the TV screen when the cable is down.

Nicholas is born on a Thursday at 9:28 p.m., just in time for our OB to get home and watch *E.R.* My husband, David, and I enter the delivery room with terrific volumes of knowledge, our heads crammed with anatomical terminology, charts, and time-lapse photography. We know how to make a baby, how to deliver a baby, how to prepare a house, a room, a car, a diaper bag for a baby's arrival. But what we never anticipated, never knew, never read in any book on what to expect, is what happens *after* you see your baby, this baby you conceived and named before meeting him. What happens inside your head full of facts and figures and misconceptions that drain like bathwater the instant you lay eyes on your child.

I was prepared to have a baby, but who or what could have prepared me for a carnal fear of loss or this love so profound it knocks the wind out of me?

It is 2 a.m., and I lie still in the dark after a one-hour bout of adrenaline shakes. I suddenly feel so small in my bed with the faint voices from the nurses' station in the hallway, so painfully aware that the safest time of this baby's life—my life—is now over. He is forever untethered.

I realize the moment I see his face for the first time that I will have to let him go in tiny, imperceptible increments every day from this moment on. A moment of incomparable regret.

There's no turning back for him. Or me.

I have crossed a new frontier. Strangely, I feel like a guest and a trespasser. This is the baby who played soccer with my spleen, the one I felt I knew so well just looking at his black-and-white sonogram. Somehow, he looked more familiar silhouetted inside my womb than he does in my arms.

Pulling out of the hospital parking lot, our It's a Boy balloon bobbing in the back window, we wave at the security guard. We are all three cocooned in fleece and down. I can see my breath. The windows are fogging. My eyes well. The sun is setting. Glancing at the hospital entrance in the side-view mirror, I remember the nurse's parting words: "Sleep him on his back. Breast milk is best. Nap when he naps. Good luck!"

On our first night, our baby son cries from 9:36 p.m. to 4:09 a.m. My heart has lodged itself in my throat, my pulse thrashing wildly as if this were the scene of a crash and I'm sifting through twisted, steaming metal until the paramedics arrive. I'm watching myself in the third person, hovering over my life. I call the doctor's office.

"If this is a life-threatening emergency, please press one . . ."

When we finally reach a pediatrician at 3:27 a.m., he instructs us to bundle up the baby and go for a drive. In the dead of night. On our *first* night. In the dead of winter.

Sitting next to him in the backseat, I can't take my eyes off his perfect face, the size of a navel orange. He is tranquil at last. We make our way back at 4:10 a.m.

4:16 a.m. Dave and I are under blankets, seconds from slumber, when the baby begins to wail hysterically. We keep blinking in the unfamiliar darkness to remind ourselves that we are not dreaming, that Nicholas is in fact real and weighs only six pounds nine ounces despite his magnificent voice. We are in a fog with this tiny gargantuan person.

We all finally get to sleep at about seven that morning. In the daylight, everything seems a little less terrifying.

Apparently, newborn infants cry when they're being changed or bathed because they instinctively feel like they're falling. Our baby must feel like he has been pushed, blindfolded, out of a Cessna, free-falling without an umbilical cord. He is frantic. He sobs when we sponge-bathe him. We try to keep him warm, to hold him, to dim the lights, to speak softly and touch him gently. I try nursing him just before his bath, even during it. We try a pacifier, but he spits it out as if a clove of garlic had just been placed on his tongue. We have actually gotten the bath down to a clean thirty seconds, enough time to wet him, dry him off, rediaper and dress him. I pretty much stop breathing during diaper changes and baths. Fortunately, both are relatively short procedures.

I had absolutely no idea that the sound of my baby's cry would affect me so deeply. I think I hear him crying when the washing machine whines in a high-pitched tone as it reaches its last cycle, or the water pipes whistle in a plaintive vibrato when the shower is running, or when the neighbor's white Persian yowls in the eaves trough above our balcony. Sometimes, I think I hear him crying when it's perfectly quiet in the house.

The crying, in and of itself, is not the central issue. It is, after all, the baby's language. It isn't even so much that I have to learn this new language. I hear his cry as more than a call for food or a diaper change. He is saying, Stop everything you're doing right now and commit to me!

It is a kind of commitment I have never known before. And it scares me numb.

I now realize that despite a university degree; a fairly extensive collection of well-thumbed books; three and a half decades of life knowledge, street smarts, and hard-won lessons; and thirteen years as a journalist and television host traveling the world, interviewing thousands of people from all walks of life—Senegalese orphans,

Holocaust survivors, war vets, Olympic athletes, mothers against drunk drivers, AIDS researchers, oncologists, movie stars, musicians, and political figures—I pretty much know nothing.

A new *mother* who knows nothing. At a time in my life when I ought to know something. Like how to console my child.

He cries. I go through a random maternal choreography with him, in search of ways to unlock the mystery of his cues. There are moments when I feel our divine symbiosis, and others when the path to each other seems hopelessly labyrinthine, an intricate maze of mixed messages and misunderstandings. How do I know if I'm right or wrong? Whom should I trust?

My husband and I take our newborn to a pediatrician, whom we chose rather arbitrarily. His practice is half a mile down the street.

"He seems to be crying a lot, especially between five and eight at night," I say to the doctor. "Is there anything we can do for him?"

"He has a little colic," says the doc, shrugging. "You have to let go and cut the umbilical cord."

A little colic? Is that like a little pregnant? Or a little married? *Let go?* I blink at the doctor; then I consult with Nicholas, his face raging with baby acne.

"Do you have children?" I ask the man.

"No," he says, grinning.

I realize at this moment that finding a pediatrician is not a random choice. Let go? Alright, if you insist.

The next baby doctor has three kids and a golden retriever.

"If you pick up the baby every time he cries, he'll cry to get picked up," he explains. "It's all conditioning."

He nods at Dave and me; then he slides his pen back into his coat pocket and closes our son's folder.

After three attempts, we eventually find a doctor, a mother of four, who takes the time to get to know our son and us. Nicholas screeches at the mere crinkling of examining-table paper, and howls desperately while she checks his ears. Still, she smiles at his beautiful, contorted face, checking his throat while his mouth is conveniently open.

"You're such a handsome little guy," she coos. "And smart, too!"

He wails and writhes, clutching my sweater like a frightened kitten.

"He's doing fine," she concludes after his first checkup.

Great, I think. Now what about *us?*

There are the books written by pediatricians, child psychologists, behavior specialists, and family therapists. There's my mother's experience and my mother-in-law's experience—a combined storehouse of eight children and seventy-nine years of parenting. There are neighbors. Friends. Strangers. And there's Public Opinion, that universal playbook that apparently applies to all babies everywhere except mine.

Then there's my feeble Gut Feeling, that faint voice calling from the bottom of the well, the so-called hunch, which may or may not qualify at this point in time as my Maternal Instinct.

And then, of course, there's the baby.

When I was pregnant, I never thought of his cry. I only prayed for a healthy baby. The ten-fingers-and-ten-toes prayer.

I never remember wishing that our baby would be the kind that slept ten hours straight. I never once prayed for proper latch-on or a good appetite or a baby who loved the stroller or traveled well. I read books about what to expect, how to achieve the optimal blanket swaddle, how to burp a baby three different ways. (Who knew?) I read about rashes, vaccines, a little about cradle cap. I knew about different poop colors and how many pee diapers meant he was getting enough milk.

But the stuff you only know about a person when you *know*

him—not his vital stats like his resting pulse and his Apgar score, but the particular way he likes to be held, his favorite perch, the spot where he burrows his face between your collarbone and shoulder tip, the way he likes to be rocked from side to side not back and forth, the sound of his sighs in triplicate just before he goes limp for the night, the subtle gradations of mood shifting across his tiny face like a cloud across a late afternoon sky, his newborn eyes still puffy and crossed, his heart-wrenching cry—these things I could never know before now.

Having a child has forced me to confront my idea of control. I realize this the moment my OB walks into the delivery room and tells me that the baby has a twenty-four-hour window to come out with his hands up or she'll have to go in after him.

In his newborn fear of falling, this child has asked me to stare long into a new life and *trust*. Myself, him, the process, God. Not an easy thing when you're used to relying on tangibles, feedback, and visual cues.

But as I lie crouched between the walls of my newborn's helplessness, it dawns on me that whatever control I thought I had over my life prior to the birth of my son was nothing more than a sleight of hand I had learned to buoy me in an uncertain world.

The days pass. I write. On napkins. Envelopes of unopened bills. Grocery receipts, unfurled white ribbons with a tidy purple price list on one side and the tiny, nearly illegible thoughts of a not entirely desperate new mother scratched in black ink on the other. I sit at the computer, tapping keys with one finger while I hold my sleeping boy in the crook of my other arm.

I write to preserve myself, my mind, memories, untamed fantasies, dueling emotions, the ancient language of pantomime between a baby and mother in the first stages of courtship. I write to lay down the tracks of the journey as we embark on our unbeaten path, placing syllables along the ground like small stones to guide me back when I need to return to the place where we started. I search for words, frames of reference, a map of new motherhood to which I can refer for reassurance and refuge.

I find, instead, that the territory is mine to chart. There is no external compass, only this baby with his sky blue eyes for arrows and his voice that sends me into the woods hunting for clues.

I write of my baby in need and his mother in conflict. I wrestle with the notion of my own competence. What do my baby's needs have to do with *my* sense of adequacy? We are now two, separated at birth. And yet, it seems impossible to ever separate our sensibilities from this moment forth.

Sometimes, when he is sleeping on my chest listening to the rhythm of my beating heart, I wonder how on earth I am ever going to have the courage to let him go. That's when free-falling feels like an eternal passage. I look at my son in these first weeks of our new life together and wonder if my feet will ever touch the ground again.

CHAPTER TWO

Breathe

don't think I have breathed since delivery. That was several weeks ago. I harbor so much doubt about "doing it right." Not by-the-book right, but rather a yearning to do right by him and for him. I keep thinking my baby might break. He is so delicate. His neck is so floppy. He is so confused about everything. How to swallow without inhaling. What to do with phlegm. Why he has to wear clothes, have his nails clipped, his belly button swabbed.

The gas thing really throws him. And me. I realize that he hasn't had much intestinal peace in these first weeks. He always seems to have that Uh-oh-I-think-I'm-gonna-hurl look on his face. I live in fear of The Hurl, because when it happens I'm convinced he has brought up all of the food he has eaten since he was born. My legs tremble while I clean him up and smile at him and sing a sweet made-up lullaby about baby spit-up.

I search my newborn's eyes for a sign that he is, you know, *happy* with me. I look at him, studying his features, his gestures, his small but impressive repertoire of reactions to my responses. And I feel like he and I have so much in common. We are both innocent, both newly born, needing to feel physically and emotionally safe with one another. I am trying to make sure he feels secure and comfortable, even though I want to curl up in the fetal position and sleep for a month. I have never been so God-help-me-tired in my life. My hair hurts.

It's the middle of the night. Dave and I take turns rocking the baby. The trick is to rock him standing up, teetering from side-to-side as opposed to back and forth. It's uncanny that such a small being can sense the difference. The moment we even *think* about inching to-ward the glider, the baby cries his bone-rattling cry of protest.

Our friends Rosemary and Eric put their baby daughter in her stroller, lay down about ten hockey sticks on their living-room car-pet, and then roll the stroller across the bumpy slats until she falls asleep.

For them it's hockey sticks; for others it's the whir of the dryer, or the purr of a vibrating bouncy seat. For us, it's side-to-side squats. I've never had better quads in my life.

People tell me to put him down.

"He'll become too attached," they reason, as if I'm *making* him dependent on me.

He makes it clear that being held is more preferable to him, right now, than lying in his baby seat, or on the floor under that red, black, and white thingie we bought to stimulate him but that only causes him acid reflux. People say I ought to let him get used to not being in my arms, to condition him to get along without me.

It's not that I want to dismiss tradition. It's just that Popular Opinion is apparently not popular with my baby. I peer into the great chasm between my intuition and the roar of the crowd. It's hard to *hear,* let alone trust, my own voice. I pick up my son, and the chorus chants "You'll spoil him." I go to him at night—"He'll never sleep on his own." I soothe him—"He'll be too dependent." I answer his call—"He'll think the world revolves around him." When he cries, he is called "difficult," while other infants are "good" babies. When I fulfill his needs, I'm "coddling him." He's the "over-indulged" baby who is bound to become the toddler "who won't take no for an answer," the dreaded "brat."

He has been out of the womb for forty-two days. And people I have never seen before in my life are laying claims on his future. On our relationship. Drawing the dividing lines. Picking sides. Home versus Visitors. Whose needs are more important—his or mine?

When people told me life was going to change, I'd balk, as if somehow I would be exempt from that fate. Your life, as you know it, will be gone forever, they'd foreshadow. And they cackled in that way voodoo witches tend to do when they are casting spells that don't rhyme and can't be undone. They said my whole focus would be different. In fact, and not to nitpick here, my entire center of *gravity* has shifted.

My senses have been sharpened. I can hear the baby's lips purse through the wall in another room. I can now see in the dark. My maternal sixth sense has been supplanted by a seventh: anticipating.

I shuffle the few steps from the bassinet to my pillow, knocking the mattress with my knees as I approach, holding my breath as I slide my toes down to the bottom of the cool sheets. I take a breath, a slow endless yawn that transports me from the day's long thread to the dream shards I remember in splintered bits that have no beginning or end and sometimes make me worry about my sanity.

I had heard about postpartum blues, though I never paid much attention to the term before. It can't be real, I thought. I remember this now as I cry over spaghetti sauce. Wrapping paper. The doorbell. My breasts. I look at the baby's toes and sob. It hurts so much to be awake. To be aware. To feel. So melancholy about his and my future. I feel like I'm mourning something, a loss. But what? My empty womb? My carefree life? The fact that I can never guarantee his safety again?

Is this my life from this moment on? Will I ever again want to stand tall and walk swiftly with my eyes on the horizon like I have a sense of direction, of purpose, of wanting to go anywhere at all? When will I not feel so self-conscious about exhaling? Will anyone notice if I never leave the house again?

These can't be the blues. Blue is the color of the sky, of the Aegean Sea, of my favorite winter turtleneck, of minty toothpaste that leaves my tongue tingling. Blue is cool and fresh. I like blue.

This is charcoal. It's the dead of night with the stars sealed behind a dome of clouds. This is muddy brown. Sepia. Mulch. Wet wood chips. Black soil. These are the colors of my postpartum rainbow. The only blue I see is in my baby son's eyes. Dark blue pools of concern darting back and forth, searching, searching.

I paw at the woolen stuffed monkey and giraffe that our neighbor Patty knitted for the baby, and I snivel into a handful of balled-up tissues. I can't believe that women have babies more than once, that my mother had three, my mother-in-law five. I cry for mothers with sick children, for mothers who have lost children, mothers of missing children. I cry for babies who are abandoned, unloved. I sob as if there has been a death in the family, not a birth. Here I am, basking in the miracle of this new person, weeping for all of humankind. Somehow, I manage to dry my eyes and compose myself in front of my son. I think he has enough on his mind after nine months of relative peace and quiet. My friend Janice assures me that I am not going crazy, that these dark clouds will soon blow away. I want to believe her.

It occurs to me that after fourteen hours of nursing rocking burping nursing changing rocking soothing washing nursing burping walking changing soothing rocking holding—after two and a half hours of uninterrupted sleep—I must do this again tomorrow and tomorrow and tomorrow.

I need to get out.

I want to take long walks with the baby, to clear my head, leave the house, change the scenery, but Nicholas is not comfortable anywhere except in my arms. I try the pouch, but by the time I strap him in, he is so distressed, I make it as far as the front door and abort the mission.

The day we actually make it outside, the sky is overcast and the air is damp. It's midafternoon and the sidewalks are barren. I walk with my baby in a forward pouch, his left ear against my chest and his belly against mine.

He sleeps.

Twenty muted minutes.

I have the feeling that I may walk forever.

The first six weeks have been a kind of hibernation. I have turned our bed into the dining-room table, the changing station, the place we nap, eat, nurse. I could put a dairy farm to shame. I just can't fathom the sheer volume of milk pouring forth from my once imperceptible breasts. They're like showerheads. I have to lie down just to slow the flow.

Every time the baby's tiny mouth approaches, I clench my jaw in anticipation of an exquisite, lingering pain. I feel hot and itchy and desperate. Guilty that I feel such dread and remorse and shame every time I hear my son's hunger cry.

I try warm compresses. Ibuprofen. Chamomile tea. Prayer. I even tried wearing chilled, uncooked cabbage leaves to relieve engorgement pain. But I just smelled like sauerkraut. Jane, the lactation nurse at the hospital, assured me that the pain would pass. I long to breastfeed my baby without flinching, or checking my watch. I try to focus on one feeding at a time. Just like him.

A week later, Ann, lactation consultant, parent educator, and mother of three well-adjusted adult children, makes a housecall. She examines my baby's latch-on and my bloody nipples. I whimper on her shoulder that I feel defective, that the baby prefers me to sit upright to feed him, and then stand up to burp him—every hour and a half at night—that my girlfriend Mercedes could actually lie down to nurse *her* baby so she still got some rest at the same time. Ann listens with terrific compassion, and then gives me an Olympian pep talk about the psychology of running a marathon.

"I feel like I'll be limping to the finish line," I sniffle.

"First of all, don't compare yourself to others. Every mother is going to have her own personal experience," she says. "And remember, this isn't a race. Nobody's timing you. Nobody's judging you. You're feeding your baby. This is between you and your child. And soon, the two of you will nurse like it's simply part of your language, a way you communicate with each other."

But when?

"A few more *weeks?*"

I swallow hard. Sometimes I feel that this baby, with all his most essential and primitive needs, could drain the life out of me. And still need more. The fact is, he needs me. And I don't want to shortchange him.

In these early weeks, I hear his cry—insistent, coded, fearful, hungry, primal, essential, urgent—and feel a quiet panic loosening my seams, reawakening all that is dormant inside me. I am this boy's mother, and yet, there are those times when I can't make it better for him. "What's wrong with him?" becomes "What's wrong with *me?*" Is he looking for something I am not giving him? Sometimes, he looks annoyed with me. Unsure. I've got to stop thinking he doesn't like me.

It might help if it was anywhere *near* acceptable to discuss any or all of these feelings honestly in public with other human beings. I have staccato conversations with people whose answers make my ears ring.

"Oh, but it's all worth it, isn't it? And he's just so adorable!"

This does wonders for my sense of isolation.

I suppose people say it's all worth it when you're at your low point because they sense you're feeling that it's not, that you're somehow regretting your decision to have conceived in the first place. But, can't a new mother feel momentarily plagued with despair *and* feel the inexorable worth of this experience, this child, this life—both at the same time?

I realize how necessary it is to find support. Being a happily married woman, I never expected to feel so alone as a new mother. This, I can see, has little to do with my husband. Somehow, sharing your struggles, confessions, and irrational fears with other mothers can be a kind of lifeline. There is nothing quite like a little old-fashioned validation from another mother who can listen without judgment, shining a light in otherwise shadowed corners.

It is *so* hard to remember this is all temporary. There are times when I feel like he will always be my tiny, miserably gassy baby, and I will always be his mother feeling his pain, stifling my panic, holding my breath. This is probably because I never imagined how hard it could be to give when you feel so tired. I never knew how different giving feels when it *isn't* reciprocal. I never knew that you just give, somehow, despite your unspeakable weariness and sense of defeat.

Giving when your cup is full feels great when you've got enough left for yourself. But giving when you've squeezed your last droplet of energy into feeding and calming the baby, when you've heaved the dry clothes on the bed in one swooping arc like a diskthrower in a decathlon, when you haven't showered or talked in full sentences for days, when you can't finish a thought, a page in a book, a hot meal—well, giving can feel downright life-threatening.

I feel humbled and intrigued that this newborn boy is teaching me how to give, how to love, how to trust, how to know him—and myself. This blessed, miraculous, wondrous, precious person has unknowingly thrust me down the well of my own life to plumb the depths of my own issues of dependency and fear and helplessness.

Sometimes, I have my hand on the horn. Not wanting to yield or merge entirely. How could I ever see in this baby's tender eyes, the wrath of El Nino? I feel sorry for having such frequent flashbacks of my former life just 1,344 hours after walking through the pearly gates of Motherhood, for taking his tears so darned personally.

I have spent the first few weeks as a new mother trembling at the crossroads of fear and love, expectation and reality, resistance and surrender. My baby urges me to stand in his chaos. In my own. To find order in it. I look in his eyes, and I see my own complexity reflected back at me.

It's raining on my birthday. The baby has been crying on and off from dawn to dusk. I nurse him, change him, rock him, sing to him, walk with him, hold him closely, whisper to him, kiss and cuddle him, but nothing has calmed him for more than a few minutes at a time. For hours, I hold him and seesaw in his favorite sideways motion, but he starts to cry the moment I stop. Eventually, he gets tired and dozes off on my shoulder, at which point I carefully recline on my bed with him. If I adjust the pillows for my comfort, he wakes up crying. I walk him back and forth from the living room down the hall to the bedroom in an endless loop, until my feet are hot and swollen.

By late afternoon, I sit on the edge of my bed with my weeping son cradled in my arms, and I do something I haven't done all day: I join him. I let the tears pour like rain. I can feel the ache fill my lungs until it begins to billow like the sails on a boat. Finally, I let it out in whispery sobs, my shoulders shaking with each wave. And suddenly, all I hear is the sound of my own voice. Nicholas is still at last, as if a switch has been flipped back to off. We silently stare at each other's wet flushed face, both of us blinking back tears.

And that's when he smiles at me. It isn't gas.

I'm absolutely positive it's a real, bona fide smile—the best birthday gift I could imagine. The rain continues well past midnight, but that smile glows like a sunrise. And, for a brief moment, I can see the horizon.

CHAPTER THREE

Blessed and Bound

'm out on the front porch on a vibrant spring morning, picking at a turkey sandwich while the baby sleeps. The forsythias have just woken up after a winter's nap, long canary yellow ribbons of bush in resplendent bloom. A light breeze catches the scent of one lone cherry-blossom tree up the hill and carries its perfume downwind to where I am.

Our postman, Larry Christmas, walks up the wooden steps to hand-deliver a package about the size of a loaf of bread. It's a gift from Lori, my best friend from high school. Inside the box is an adorable red, white, and blue striped baby overall and hat she knitted for Nicholas.

Lori's note says, "Do not despair! Eight weeks approaches fast!"

How did she know I was desperate for some marker, a flare on the road to let me know where I might be?

The blues are pretty much done with me. Several eternal weeks of dense postpartum clouds poured without letup. Dave could only stand by and watch, helpless and anxious, alternately sympathetic and impatient.

"This will pass," he would reassure me. *"Won't it?"* he'd sometimes add, hoping for an affirmative answer.

These days, my blues are more shades of pale gray. There are times when I am filled with such divine gratitude for the very existence of this little boy. Then, there are moments when I wonder if I'll have enough energy to sustain us both.

I feel privileged and trapped at the same time. Blessed and bound.

Sometimes, I catch myself wishing the baby would hurry and grow, hold his own bottle, sit upright in his own chair, walk. But then I imagine him boarding a little yellow school bus, his cartoon knapsack on his shoulders, flashing me his impish smile from the window, and my chest tightens.

I'm caught between the baby and the boy, fear and faith, hoping for a smooth ride for both of us. I wish I could guarantee his safety forever, though I know I can't, and I fight that fact daily as though I'm leaning into a strong wind and losing.

When he's asleep, I embrace the silence, the stillness of doing nothing. For a moment, I feel such deep relief because my hands are free. I can write. I can make a snack, open mail, have a shower, return a phone call. But soon, I begin to feel distracted by the silence.

I peek through the crack of the door into the room where he is napping. The sight of his small face, his soft flower lips, his boyfingers curled into baby fists like he's holding something special in his palm—a seashell or a candy—somehow breaks my heart: I cannot imagine feeling a deeper love for and devotion to any living creature on earth, yet I feel a strange sort of betrayal. The silence has lured me into its fold for a few brief moments, then filled itself with emptiness. I can't hear the quiet now without feeling the longing.

I stare at his feet a lot. I gaze, bleary-eyed, at his Flintstone feet in the moonlight, his big toes pointing skyward, his slivered toenails looking more like clippings than nails.

He is sprawled across me like a blanket. I nurse him in the rocker by the window. The pain is gone now. In fact, I think I can vouch for Nicholas when I say that he and I can scarcely remember the weeks of agony and anxiety that preceded this moment. Now when he nurses, he occasionally hooks his fingers onto my tank top like he's riding the subway and that's his strap.

I drift in and out of sleep while he suckles, half-dreaming that I had a baby. Here, in our cocoon of impenetrable security, I don't want to think of bike helmets and designated drivers. I don't want to think of scraped knees and curfews. I don't want to think of the wrong crowd, the heartbreak that sends him reeling. Right now, all I really worry about is gas. Will that bubble that I didn't manage to get out wake him in the middle of the night?

I think we're getting our routine down a little better every hour, every day. Sometimes it feels as if we actually have a rhythm, and some days it feels like mayhem.

"He's getting organized," says Rebecca, my OB, at my six-week postpartum check-up. *He's getting organized.* What a brilliant alibi! It lifts the burden right off me and my baby to feel—or be—any different than we are right now. We are *both* getting organized. I'm trying hard not to let my baby's tears make me weak in the knees. Just be there, I keep thinking. He just wants me to show up. Answer the call.

But sometimes I can't decipher the call, and I feel dumb-founded, dumb, numb with helplessness. I get a sense that his language is more profound than words and I'm still weighed down by clumsy vocabulary.

After I feed him, I hoist him onto my left shoulder. His eyes are closed, his belly filled, and there he hangs in his Charlie Brown way, arms by his side, his cheek to my shoulder, the last weary couple at the dance marathon. Our chests rising and falling together, his almost twice as fast as mine. I cup his foot in my palm and gently stroke his heel, as silken as a polished stone. I wear him like a priceless stole I never want to take off, listening for the succession of breaths—heavy triplets, sixteenth and eighth notes—until his breath is so shallow I can barely hear it.

"Does it hurt when I do this?" asks the physical therapist.

I don't make a habit of yelling in public places, but this pain is so bad that I have recently started dropping napkins and cotton balls because of their sheer weight.

"DeQuervain's syndrome," says the woman who looks twelve even though she has three children in school. "It's from holding the baby in the same way for long periods of time, like during nursing. Think carpal tunnel."

Rest the hand, she advises, and then instructs me to wear a splint on my hand and wrist that immobilizes my thumb. For two weeks. Is she kidding me? Change a diaper, nurse, make meals, drive a car with one hand?

In the middle of a diaper change, my son looks up at me with a face that seems to say, "What's with the slo-mo, Ma? I thought you had this down already."

A few weeks after Nicholas's birth, I can only vaguely recall the curve of my belly, how it felt to massage the bumps where he kicked and changed positions.

I find it so difficult to relax as a new mother, even when there is a reprieve. This is not due to my fatigue or the relentlessness of caretaking, but rather to the long string of intangibles I tie around my finger that remind me constantly of his fragility—and mine. The vulnerable child within me begins to ask with quiet shame, What about *me?* What about *my* aches and pains and worries? Who will take care of *me?*

How does a new mother stay in the moment and keep her eye on the horizon at the same time?

I have things to learn from this baby. Life lessons. Big marquee blinking, ah-ha moments no therapist or pastor or pediatrician could reveal to me. Nearly two months old, my son stays in the moment so well. He has no awareness of what's to come, no concern about the next meal or diaper change. His needs are current, unencumbered by expectation. I envy his lack of defense, his motivations devoid of yearning and regret, his simplicity of desire. He doesn't second-guess himself—or me.

I hear my baby's siren song between dusk and dawn. I lumber through the shadows of our bedroom with a kind of melancholy. There's no audible conversation at that hour. In the solitude of overnight feedings, it's just me and the boy in the dark.

Really, it's just *me* in the dark. Nicholas won't remember any of this. He'll never know how persistently I tried to get that bubble up, how gently I rocked him and kissed the nape of his neck before laying him down to sleep.

Everything I did before this has faded to black. I once knew other things. Now, I know this baby. I know him in the way that a person knows anything after so much time and energy have been invested. In my overnight haze, I feel so solitary; all I can do is look at my baby and memorize his form before he outgrows it.

It's a double bind. Intimacy and loneliness. Connection and separateness. Wanting to be with him and wanting a moment alone. Wanting to fulfill his needs and feeling overwhelmed by them. Wanting to stay home with him and wanting to forge my own path in the world. Loving him so deeply and fearing his loss, my loss.

How can I feel an iota of hopelessness during a time of such hope? How can a time of such bonding feel binding?

I stand in the shower between the curtain and the tiles with my prickly loofah, sloughing off dead skin and contradictions. Trying to wash my ambivalence down the drain. I have about a minute and a half to loiter, not quite enough time to steam up the entire bathroom mirror. After a shower, I have this feeling of starting over, a cleansing on many levels. Like this shower is the line between chaos and sanity, despair and hope.

Baby wakes up crying after a thirty-minute snooze. I stand under the waterfall for an extra three seconds before my thumb jabs the faucet back into the wall, wondering if my ambivalence is here to stay. I realize that as a mother I won't always have the answers.

Maybe the contradictions are about learning to live with and accept some degree of duality and ambiguity. Maybe ambivalence is patience in disguise. Maybe it's a rest stop, a detour, a scenic drive. Part of the journey.

Maybe standing at a fork in the road is a moment of grace, not just a time of choice.

Nicholas sleeps ten hours straight on May eleventh, a date I want to frame and hang on the wall, the day I win the sleep lottery, the day he awakes rested and content and flashes me the fattest smile I ever saw, the day I can finally see tomorrow.

Overnight, I go from feeling shackled and forsaken to feeling free, motivated, hopeful, and inspired. Even though I am still jolted awake by breasts that have a life and time zone of their own. Still, after ten minutes of pumping at 2 a.m., I don't have to burp them and rock them back to sleep, so already I can see some improvement in the general scheme of things.

Then again, maybe improvement is too strong a word. But when you're eager for a beacon, something to give you a sense of direction—of progress—it's difficult *not* to think in terms of improvement.

I think of Lori's note. How that eight-week marker feels like a mirage, something so abstract and impossible. How a figure eight is burned into my mind, skywritten across the clear blue, making way for a giant scrim to descend from the rafters designating the end of act one.

CHAPTER FOUR

Mother Me

hen my mother flies down to meet her first grandchild, he is ten days old, and she is scheduled to visit for three weeks. After she arrives, we push her departure date across the calendar like a bead on an abacus. She'll leave, we all agree, after the baby sleeps through the night, after his second vaccine, after his acne clears up, after my breasts stop aching, after she senses, as only a mother can, that I am no longer desperately in need of rest.

It isn't a smooth ride.

There are complexities in being a firstborn-daughter-turned-new-mother in the face of a mother-turned-new-grandmother. I want guidance, but not advice. My mom wants me to feel good when my body has been bungee jumping without the cord, to be happy when I'm weeping over junk mail. I want to trust my intuition—which at this point I still haven't quite located—and my mother wants me to trust her experience.

Even though my mother gave birth three times, I still feel the need to teach her how to burp a baby.

"Hold him like *this*, Mom!"

"Oh my God! You're choking him!"

"Mom, you hold him at the jaw not the neck."

"I always just patted your *back.*"

"Just *try* the jaw hold."

"Look! Just hold him upright and he burps on his own!"

This is lighthearted banter.

I don't know how much I can blame my hormones for siphoning off every last vestige of patience I may have had in my previous incarnation as a rational woman who still had bladder control. I'd like to blame them entirely. In fact, I think I will.

The baby cries his raw, helpless, raise-the-dam cry, the one where I worry about his future as an angst-ridden, antisocial person who feels nobody understands him except the squirrels on the roof of his log cabin deep in the woods.

I hear the cry and feel it in my bones. I sense his anger, his dissatisfaction with me as his mother. Until my own mother provides translation—or tries to, anyway.

"He's not angry, he's hungry!" she declares.

"But he seems so adamant," I reason remorsefully.

"He knows what he wants! It's fantastic!"

"But he gets so mad if he doesn't eat immediately."

"He has a wonderful appetite! God bless him!"

Weeks later, we have a similar exchange:

"He gets so upset if he doesn't get what he wants."

"He has a will," she explains. "It's great!"

"But he seems . . . demanding."

"He has a will, but not the capacity. You know how *frustrating* that is for him?" she asks.

And of course, my personal favorite: "He's *exactly* like *you* were as a baby!"

My mom says this with a wonderful mix of reassurance, genetic reverence, nostalgia, and a twist of lime. At first, it comforts me. Then a queasiness overtakes me. I have something to learn from the comparison. Something to learn from my discomfort with it. If Nicholas and I are so similar and there are things I don't like, I have to confront the fact that I don't like them in myself. He is teaching me about the subtle ways we reject ourselves, how we can turn a cold shoulder to the things we don't like within us, shutting them out of view, erecting an invisible wall where there once was a sore spot. The same wall that stands between us and our children.

My mother is over the moon about her first grandchild. She loves to watch him exist. He sleeps, and she shakes her head. "He's unbelievable," she gushes. "Just look at those lips, those eyelashes. Listen to how he breathes. It's like music!" She calls him "agapi," which means "my love" in Greek.

Within hours of her arrival, our home is redolent with the familiar aroma of chicken strips sauteed with garlic, broccoli, and red peppers; cheesy pasticcio; spanakopita folded in crispy phyllo triangles; and tender baklava with crushed walnuts. I eat without lifting my head from the plate, as though I haven't seen food in months. My mother stocks the freezer, folds towels, makes fruit salad, and when I am seized with the flu, offers me hot chicken soup and a cool cloth for my head. She lives to give.

Nicholas is almost three months old. Dave and I drag our feet through the house, brushing the walls with slouched shoulders. My mother wants to help, so she offers to get up with the baby at night. At this point, I remind her that my breasts are leaking. She then encourages me to pump and give her a bottle of breast milk so that she can relieve me of at least one feeding. I explain how uncomfortable I become if I don't nurse, how the pump expresses only some of the milk, how *much* milk I produce, and so forth. I then launch into a one-minute harangue about nipple confusion, and my mother looks at me like I have three breasts. After several spirited discussions, I agree to let her give the baby some bottled breast milk for an overnight feeding while I attempt to get an extra two hours of sleep.

Nicholas cries at 2:34 a.m. I open my eyes, hear my mother go to him, hear him gulping his milk, hear her patting his back, hear the baby belch, and listen drowsily to the whispery sonnets of a Greek lullaby.

Kyo pou toh poh nee ny ah nee (Wherever it hurts let it heal)
Nah nee nah nee nah nee nah. (Sleep sleep sleep)

She sings both the baby and me back to sleep. In two hours, my breasts are the size of Texas. My mother is trying to establish a routine, and I am anxious that her routine will disrupt mine. She accuses me of being neurotic. I accuse her of trying to stage a coup. And we call it a night.

I am feeling hot flashes of self-doubt about my ability to soothe my own child. I have a silly superstition that the baby is sleeping the night because of something my mother is doing. Some kind of magic touch that only his grandmother possesses. He is so peaceful in her arms. As her departure looms, I feel anxious about continuity. What if he doesn't sleep the night with *me?* What if I don't have her . . . magic touch?

I never thought my defenses would be working as hard as my milk ducts. As a new mother in the face of my own mother's teachings, I admit I have not always been a willing student.

How could she know my baby like I know my baby? I *know* he's hungry! She thinks I don't know he's hungry? What does she think, I'm going to let him starve? Of course he's tired! *I* know that cry! *I* know how to comfort my own baby!

I can feel the ancient pangs of adolescence.

———

The sky is dark. My mother is in the kitchen sterilizing baby bottles in a glass pot of bubbling water on the stove. She takes a moment to check in with the baby and me in the bedroom, and we get to talking. Nearly an hour later, the acrid stench of burnt plastic fills the house. In minutes, the kitchen is filled with smoke, and the alarm goes off in the hallway. We scramble around the house, my mother rushes to the kitchen, I throw on a coat, snatch the baby, tuck him inside it, and dash out the door, down the icy front steps to seek refuge in our heated car. I can smell burnt bottles from the driveway. I see my mother standing on the frosty balcony in a black T-shirt on a bitter cold night. She has spotted me and the baby, past the snowcapped bushes huddled in the passenger seat of our parked car. For a moment, I am the mother looking at my daughter fidgeting on the front porch in anticipation of her imminent punishment.

She is the outsider; I am the all-knowing parent.

She is the absentminded teenager; I am the sage, wise mother who looks upon her with indignation and pity, wanting to both chastise and forgive her.

And, suddenly, I remember the night she let me borrow her brand-new coat. I was seventeen. It was her first fancy coat, a full-length dark brown suede coat with faux fur on the collar and a suede belt that cinched at the waist—a coat she could have never imagined as a little girl growing up, crouched with her mother in their basement during World War II air raids. A coat she would have never dreamed she'd ever wear, let alone own, when she was forty-seven. I put the coat on and slipped my hands into its deep, satin pockets. I felt like a princess despite my frizzy hair and monobrow. I nodded impatiently as she reminded me to drive carefully, to be home early. I was on my way out when she warned me about the freshly painted walls in the vestibule by the front door—she wasn't sure they were completely dry. As I rushed to leave, I brushed against the wall, smearing a four-inch stroke of white semigloss on the brand-new brown suede coat she had not yet worn. She said nothing at the time. I never knew her disappointment until a decade later when she confessed it in passing one day when we were cleaning out her front-hall closet and unearthed the coat.

On this night years later, I sit in the car with my baby, watching the windows fog and my mother freeze. I'm on the inside. She's on the outside.

Forgiveness hangs in the balance.

I want to comfort her, let her off the hook, laugh about molten plastic. I want to let her know that I am grateful she is here, ready to love me and this new baby so much, insisting that I sleep another hour at the crack of dawn.

And I want to sit here in the car all night, all week, cocooned with my child at my bosom, where I can hear myself think and just maybe trace the sound of my own maternal voice. I want to imagine the impossible ease of motherhood, the courage of parenting with relaxed conviction instead of defense.

I realize the complexity of wanting to be a new mother who doesn't need my mother while also wanting to be a new mother of whom my mother can be proud. I am weighed down by the pain of wanting both to mother and be mothered at a time when I feel vulnerable and scared.

I want her to go away and stay close. I want her to give me room to find my way, and I want to let her teach me something about motherhood.

When I come back inside the house with my baby tucked inside my coat, my mother looks remorseful, embarrassed, guarded, guilty, innocent, concerned. I feel exactly the same way. I am fully prepared to let it go, to burst out laughing.

But instead something vile bubbles up from the well, and I shake my head in contempt, mumble derisively under my breath. It isn't about burnt bottles. I have turned my own mother into the enemy faction, seeing her involvement as interference, misperceiving her help as control, her suggestions as criticism, and her criticism as disapproval of me as a mother. I have placed squarely on my mother's shoulders the entire burden of my legitimacy as a parent, as a person. We have time-traveled back to a time, when I wanted to do it myself and she wanted to spare me the agony of defeat.

On this winter night with my newborn, I realize that it's not so much that I want to do it myself, but that I want to experience *all* of it—the triumph and the struggle, the victories and failures. I have been resisting my mother's efforts at helping me pave my path. She wants a smooth road for her daughter, and I want to feel the gravel along the way. I want to take the detours. I want to find the compass within. I want to feel the pride of self-mastery.

I want her to let go. I want to compare notes, not fight over whose way works better. But instead of telling her how I feel, I am swept downstream by my own fears.

It's 3 a.m. The bottles are on the back porch still in the pot, three bottles now melted down to one charred glob, nipples twisted, jutting and melded like a school science project gone terribly wrong. The house now smells more like somebody burned dinner earlier in the evening.

I nurse my baby in the rocker. My mother sits to my left, squatted on the wooden turtle footstool my mother-in-law, Joan, hand-painted when Nicholas was born. The room is lit only by a two-inch yellow night-light plugged into the wall socket on the other side of the room. We look like Girl Scouts around campfire embers, sitting in silence, with the dark night wrapped around our shoulders. My defenses have been melted by post midnight fatigue. Everything seems fragile at this hour. My mother gazes at me and my baby.

"This is what I've lived my whole life for," she whispers woozily.

After clashing by day over roles and rules, my instincts versus her experience, my mother eases my solitude in the dead of night. The turtle hears it all, our misunderstandings, confessions, our dreams.

We sit by the night-light while the baby suckles, and we sort things out. She needs to feel needed, and I need to feel competent. She wants me to benefit from her experience, and I long to have my own. She wants me to know where she came from, who she was when I was born, what she expected and dreamed of, what broke her heart and what filled her soul. She watches me with my new son, sees the way I press my cheek to his, feels the unspeakable love I have for him, and she can't help but relive snapshots of her past, yearn to share her wisdom, her own pilgrimage. It isn't until this night that I learn of the numbing despair she suffered in her first year with three children under the age of four, how my dad's mother watched over us one morning while my mom, feeling hopeless and isolated, drove twenty-five miles to the International Expo to wander the busy grounds for two hours, wearing the massive crowds like a tight-knit shawl.

It dawns on me that she was once in my shoes—vulnerable, sleep-deprived, overwhelmed, battling ambivalence, loneliness, doubt—and that she has traveled a long, long way, bearing witness to so much more than teething pain and diaper rash.

We whisper about the importance of making our own mistakes, working out the threads of our own tangles, and weaving our own patchwork quilt that bears our hard-won lessons.

As she speaks, I imagine her as a new mother *without* a mother thirty-seven years ago. I think about how difficult it must have been for her to go through this rite of passage. Without her own mother's map for background information, historical perspective, and context, she had an immense void where I do not.

I have been wishing for my mother to let go, and yet the thought of letting *her* go makes my heart ache. I realize the value in our conflicts, how they have challenged me to redefine my perceptions, tap my inner resources, trust my gut, dismantle my defenses. And I appreciate how they have challenged my mother to see me as a mother and not just her baby, to let my experience and choices exist separately from hers.

What chasm of steel nerve and lost opportunity might otherwise divide a mother and daughter, keeping them forever at bay?

I want to thank her. For being here. For being there. For being. For making all my birthday cakes from scratch.

Now I realize that sometimes the way to find your own way is to just get out of it. I can see myself in my mother as she sees herself in me. Between our mirror images is a new reflection. I remind myself of this when she forgets the boiling bottles again a week later and the house fills with acrid fumes.

And I remind myself again when I burn them the next day in an empty house while my mother and the baby are out for an afternoon walk.

CHAPTER FIVE

Strolleritis

hen I was pregnant, I had these lovely visions of strolling the baby for hours through Central Park, winding through the streets of Soho, chatting with artisans, stopping at an outdoor market for mangoes. I imagined stashing fruit in the underbelly of the stroller, placing a smoothie in the cup holder, walking in no particular hurry while the baby snoozed in the buggy with the lid down to shield his face from the sun.

Funny how reality enjoys a good confrontation with our expectations.

What makes one baby different from another is coded somewhere in the double helixes or subject to circumstance, geography, parental responses, diet, lighting, traffic, inclement weather, the Dow Jones, or whether the lint trap was cleaned between laundry loads. In other words, who really knows?

At this point in my life, our big adventure is a trip to the mailbox, a whole hundred yards from our front porch. I travel all the way there with the baby, whom I can wear in a pouch now without incident, as long as he's facing outward like a baby kangaroo. We walk behind the house along the winding path with the willow trees, Nicholas's dangling legs perpetually pedaling. I point out the birdfeeders, swat away menacing insects, and croon made-up songs on an endless loop.

I read him all the mail, even the bills, narrating the event like Steve from *Blue's Clues* commentating at a PGA Open, opening the little metal door in slow motion complete with cartoon sound effects.

"Please . . . remit payment . . . as so-oo-on as possible . . . to maintain . . . se-ervice." (Insert a few bars of the *Pink Panther* theme here for personal amusement.)

My lower back is killing me.

Why isn't this big bruiser of a baby sitting pretty in his fetching new stroller? He's allergic to it. No kidding. My husband and I have dubbed this mysterious condition "strolleritis." The moment Nicholas even catches a glimpse of the handsome vessel—which we carefully selected because it had a cup holder on the handlebar—he becomes visibly agitated. Inside of thirty seconds in the seat, he is overcome by a kind of fight-or-flight distress that sends his limbs into near apoplexy. He shakes uncontrollably while he coughs and gasps for air.

We have asked him on several occasions exactly why he is strollerphobic, but he just stares at us blankly.

The car isn't any better. On a good day, we can make the five-mile drive to our pediatrician's office without trauma. Often, we turn on the ignition, and Nicholas begins to howl as if he is in restraints, handcuffed and bucking, like we never read him his rights, never let him make that one phone call. It isn't petty resistance; he is barely sixteen weeks old. It's usually gas, so the only solution is to pull over, unbuckle him, and remove him promptly. By the time I am cradling his bald head under my chin, baby sobs eclipsing his breath, I am wasted. And *there's* the burp.

"Maybe he's got motion sickness," suggests our baby's doctor.

"Could be the straps," offers the nurse who weighs him.

"What about the angle of the seat in the car and in the stroller?" wonders my mother.

"You're not serious!" friends blurt annoyingly after I make the mistake of sharing our anticar, antistroller plight.

"That's weird. Our baby loved the car. We drove to Canada. He slept the whole way! And he just loves the stroller! We go out every night for an hour before bedtime."

It's hard to smile at, even respond to, stories of baby mobility when you've worn shoe-tracks in the rug.

I have also made the mistake of calling a friend who had her baby girl two months after I had my son.

"I can take her anywhere!" she squeals.

The room seems to get smaller.

"She loves the car, loves the stroller, and puts herself to sleep," she continues.

I feel more than a mounting annoyance toward her.

"She can entertain herself for an hour in her bouncy seat," she adds. "And she hardly ever cries. I tell my husband all the time that we have the perfect baby."

I thoroughly dislike her for a few satisfying minutes.

I have completely lost sight of the fact that soon Nicholas will be begging me for a skateboard, and strolleritis will be a vague, sweet memory.

When I'm surrounded by babies in strollers everywhere I turn—*sleeping* babies in strollers pushed nonchalantly by parents browsing through Wal-Mart and unfazed by fluorescent lights and noise and the time of day—it's easy to forget Nicholas is going to grow up and grow out of his mysterious aversions. Instead, I stare like a tourist without a camera trying to take in a world wonder.

We try to venture out with the baby on small journeys. A trip to the grocery store is a family outing. Dave drives, and I sit in the back with Nicholas, playing it cool, wearing Disney smiles as if we do this all the time, behaving as if he loves the moment we hoist the stroller out of the trunk and snap it into position on the pavement. One of the things I admire about our son is that he is not one for pretense. He can see right through the act. Just in case we forgot about strolleritis, he is always good enough to remind us.

During the week, if I have to run errands, I do so after dinner when I can leave the baby with Dave and bolt to the grocery store where I can be seen scurrying in and out of the aisles like a rabid animal, tossing things in my cart just as those TV contestants do on that supermarket game show.

When Dave calls in during the day to see how the baby and I are doing, we usually cover the stroller issue first, as pressing as any headline story on the evening news.

"Well?" he prompts.

"Thirteen minutes," I say, in our stroller code language.

"Impressive."

One early evening, Dave and I take Nicholas out in the stroller for a brief jaunt when something astonishing happens: he falls asleep. We wear drunken grins for the rest of the walk, which lasts forty-five supernal minutes. This has happened only twice, enough for us to file it under Mere Coincidence.

I am well on my way to believing that Nicholas is the only human baby with acute strolleritis when I meet Melissa. Melissa's daughter Keaton, born a few months before Nicholas, apparently hated the stroller and car seat for the first six months of her life.

I feel light-headed, a happy, warm-footed buzz. I want to hear every detail. Melissa says they went nowhere for six months, stayed home or close to it, trying to get out a little every day, until Keaton's six-month birthday—when strolleritis suddenly disappeared.

I want to prick my finger and make the woman my blood sister.

Maybe, Dave and I muse, when Nicholas can sit upright in the stroller, buckled in at the waist and not reclined in the snap-on car seat on top the stroller, which requires over-the-shoulder straps and a buckle between his legs, maybe *then* he'll like the stroller, that

ATV of a stroller, the mother of all strollers, whose tires look as new as they did in the store.

One day, in his fourth month of life, on a spectacular day in June, I decide that I will take Nicholas out in the stroller every morning and afternoon. Even if it's for a daily grand total of forty-two seconds.

I try to be swift about it, scat-singing a jazzy ditty about how we are going out in the stroller-oller-oller and he is going to like it, like it, like it, as I am easing the straps over his head, buckling him in, and locking the front door, while his eyes are fixed intently on the exaggerated movements of my mouth. Before we know it, we are moving, sandwiched between baking asphalt and a cerulean sky, my hands actually *on* the handle of the stroller in a pushing way and Nicholas actually *in* the stroller in a sitting way, both of us traveling along the sidewalk, by the fire hydrant with the red and white chipped paint, next to the aluminum mailboxes, by the cars parked side by side hugging the long slab of a curb in front of the gray clapboard condos, the stroller wheels squeaking as they roll toward the wall of trees hiding the stretch of Interstate 95 at the end of the street, past the balcony railing lined in red geraniums, catching glimpses of other strollers in the distance, feeling part of the stroller universe, participating, gaining ground, now further from our front door than ever before, over the grooves and cracks in the cement, bumping across sewer slats, around giant garbage cans that make a hideous racket when the truck lifts them up off the ground and hurls their contents into its mouth like a big, stinking dinosaur of steel, strolling along, strolling down the block, riding with the wind, flying, gliding, soaring, breathing in our freedom for sixteen extraordinary minutes. I am studying Nicholas studying the clouds and the hubcaps, his hands on his knees, his bottom lip tucked in, his brow slightly furrowed, furrowing a little more, his lips turning downward now, his hands twitching, his head writhing from side to side, his breathing more erratic, his eyes little baby pools, spilling, wetting his cheeks, while I do a soft-shoe before him, smiling, jogging, clapping, pointing to hubcaps and clouds and garbage cans, trying to quickly gauge, as I blow him kisses and sing my what's-the-matter song, if he's bored or in pain or tired or hungry, unbuckling him, easing the straps over his scalp, rocking him while his tears stop, his body relaxes, his head rests on my left shoulder, as I prod the newly evacuated stroller with my right hand, to the back of the dim, musty garage, whisper-singing the stroller-oller-oller song, out of breath now, climbing the wooden stairs to our front door, feeling distinctly, if faintly, encouraged.

CHAPTER SIX

Grandstanding at the Shallow End

bout a hundred yards down the hill from our door is the neighborhood pool, a rectangular blue box surrounded by a brigade of strollers parked on the grass. I walk through the wrought-iron gates with my five-month-old son perched inside a Snugli and scan the pool area for an available chair. I mistake a pool mother's waving arm for an invitation when I realize she is signaling the pizza delivery boy toward her as though he were a small aircraft and she were the hangar.

Reclining women—pool mothers—chat across two or three empty chairs. They are quick to inquire about other babies' habits, preferences, teeth, and sleep patterns and, in turn, to talk about *their* baby's habits, preferences, teeth, and sleep patterns. We can share the most intimate details of our deliveries, our third-degree tears, our cracked nipples, our babies' bowel movements, and yet never know each other's name.

Nicholas begins to cry, and suddenly a deeply tanned woman wearing a purple bikini and matching toenails whispers to me from an adjacent pool chair that she considered dropping her baby off their balcony during the highest octave of his inconsolable colic. She can admit that now, she says, now that her son is applying for college. Despite her homicidal fantasies, I like her. At least, she isn't grandstanding.

"How old?" asks another pool mother, pointing to my baby with her nose. She queries me from her reclined position, squinting behind her opaque sunglasses. Her dark hair is twisted in a clip behind her head, her ten-month-old baby asleep in the stroller nearby.

"Nicholas is five mon—"

"Sleeping the night?" she asks.

"Well, he was from about six weeks, but then he started teething a month ago, so he's—"

"My daughter has all her teeth, so we're over that hump. She sleeps pretty much seven to seven. She *loves* to sleep. She's a really good baby. What about him? Is he *good*?"

Good means "doesn't cry." Sleeps a lot. Convenient. Comes into the fold without stirring things up too much.

Like my neighbor's new dog.

"Zeke's really good," Rob says. "He hardly barks at all."

The good baby is otherwise known as the "easy baby." Easy is a misnomer. I mean, Ted Bundy may well have been an easy baby.

Anyway, the day is oppressively hot and humid. I am in shorts and a cotton tank top. I've stripped Nicholas down to his number-four diaper. We are huddled in the corner by the shrubs, nursing, our stomachs glued to each other with sunscreen and sweat. I hear a mother a few feet from us talking to her child under the pool tent.

"Shhhhh!" she insists, half-leaning into the navy blue stroller where her infant is lying on his back. "Be quiet!" she barks in a loud whisper. "You make it sound like you're being *tortured*!"

A baby's cry makes us uncomfortable. If it's someone else's baby, we either smile at the mother sympathetically like it's not her fault, or contemptuously like it *is* her fault. If it's our own baby, we feel uneasy with the baby's discomfort—and our own.

There are those times when I feel inadequate if I can't console my baby, anxious and guilty that he might be unhappy. Angry that I feel vulnerable and inadequate and guilty. Ashamed that I feel angry.

It's easier, I think, for us to see the baby as difficult or fussy than to confront all these feelings in ourselves. "Good" babies don't provoke these feelings in us. Good babies go with the flow. Good babies make us feel good about ourselves—so we feel good about *them*.

At the front gate near the soda machine, a three-week-old baby is trying to cry. In this scorching heat, I think he is too woozy to let out a wail with any conviction. His mother, sunburned shoulders slouched, pushes him slowly in the stroller.

"He's awfully cranky today; I don't know why," she says to me, mopping the sweat from her forehead with the clean end of her burp pad as she slides four quarters into the coin slot for her frosty Diet 7-Up.

"You nursing?" a pool mother asks me out of the clear blue. She's not really reading her *New York Times,* just rustling the pages. We are sitting upright on reclined chairs under the blue and white striped awning, a tattered and faded flag waving at the top of the pole behind her head on the other side of the pool fence.

I nod. Nicholas stares at her.

"I nursed for two weeks," she shakes her head, "but my daughter didn't latch on well because I have inverted nipples."

Now, we've been interacting for more than ten minutes, basically discussing our breasts, and I haven't a clue who this woman is. The thought crosses my mind as she continues talking that I probably will never know, and that for this moment, this conversation, we will just continue to discuss our breasts and probably our pelvic floors and then be on our way.

We did, and we were.

It's the strangest of bonds. The conversation among new mothers is personal, often in hushed tones, and feels like the first stages of courting. Lots of questions, giggles, knowing glances, I've-been-there smiles. But just when I feel a wave of familiarity wash over me, it backs down, retreating to its previous anonymity.

Sometimes, after a fairly lengthy exchange with a mother I've met for the first time, she'll wish me good luck as Nicholas and I are leaving. I know in that instant that she won't remember my name next time. The "good luck" mothers get everything covered on the first visit so that the next time they say hello, there's nothing more to say. They have the polite and acknowledging wave down pat. A sort of discreet, economical Queen Elizabeth wave that could never hail a cab in Manhattan. An understated movement that lets you know you have been spotted, but only because you saw her first.

There are the mothers who grandstand, not about their baby's accomplishments, but their own. One first-time mother explains to me (and anyone else within earshot) how she got her five-month-old son to sleep through the night.

"I let him cry," she says, standing by the pool steps, one foot perched on the silver ladder railing. "Fifteen minutes straight. Hysterical crying," she adds, slapping her thigh with her wet palm, which startles two crows off a nearby tree branch.

"I mean, frantic screaming," she explains. "After three nights, he stopped. He has been sleeping the night ever since."

I stare at her three fingers frozen in some kind of Girl Scout salute. She stabs her fingers into her hair, and gives her curls a shake as if to wake them up.

"I know, I know. It's really hard," she adds. "But I did it. Look, if you can't do it, you can't do it! It's very hard to take, but I did it. And it worked."

I am standing before her at the steps to the shallow end with my baby in a pouch, and I want to say something. I want to howl interminably about how pitiful I think it is to let a baby bawl himself into exhaustion alone in the dark. I want to lift the flaps of auburn hair from her ears and shout, "What are you *talking* about, woman? This child is twenty weeks old! He was in the *womb* longer than he's been out here! He has gas! He has a hangnail! He's thirsty! He's lonely! He's disoriented! His incisors are coming in! His Velcro diaper tab is pinching his thigh! And you want to teach him how to *sleep*? He wants comfort for things you can't see! *Can't you see?*"

But I manage to say, "Phew! Hot out, huh?"

And I think that's about it. I don't want to judge. Really, I don't. Besides, she's bigger than I am, and I can imagine her decking me in a split second, my nose bloody, my back on the wet cement, and there, towering over me, would be this woman wringing out her fingers and letting me cry it out.

I guess I couldn't let Nicholas scream hysterically alone in the dark, because I think of all the trust he has built in us to respond to him. This pool mother has broken her son's night-waking pattern. But if I did that to my baby, I feel like I'd be breaking *him*.

I yearn to talk with another mother. I want to swap stories, not stats. I want to tell someone how cooped up I feel these days, how frustrated and odd and sad I feel that my baby has a mysterious allergy to his stroller, that we don't go anywhere further than a five-mile radius by car. I want someone to see that even though he cries and doesn't sleep fourteen hours straight and doesn't giggle like a Gerber baby every time a stranger tickles his wattle, that he isn't a good baby or a bad baby but just a baby—my magnificent baby.

I want someone to stop seeing my child within the hard, unforgiving margins of a category and say something instead about the knowingness in his knit brow, the beauty in his intensity, the brilliance in his fussiness. I want someone to give me a small parcel of hope, some perspective, to remind me of the big picture. I want to tell someone about how heavy my heart feels by midday, between his naps and laundry loads, when the phone isn't ringing, when I am feeling small and forgotten, while he sleeps so deeply in my arms, or as I'm finishing our fourth lap around the block. I really want somebody to ask me how I'm *feeling,* but instead we talk about feeding and schedules and birth weight and whose baby is rolling over first, and I feel more alone than before I came through the gates.

A few weeks later, a pool mother appears who doesn't stand at the shallow end, but instead sits over by the deep end with her baby in her arms. I wave to her as Nicholas and I approach for a visit. She is holding her baby in one arm and pushing the stroller with the other hand. Tall with fine sandy hair cut to her collarbone, she moves slowly since her caesarean section three weeks ago. She has just given birth to her second daughter.

"How are you, Donna?" I ask as we get closer.

"Ohhhhh," she keens, "I needed to get out."

Indoor caretaking has a way, as any new mother can attest, of throwing into question the meaning of the term "daylight." Even the characteristics of daylight—the light, for one—get shmushed into that hazy place in the back of one's mind, which to the new mother begins to resemble the floor behind the fridge where we never sweep.

"She just won't be put down. She cries every time we lay her in the bassinet," Donna says, barely audibly. "I literally have to hold her all the time."

The woman's singing my song. I want to wrap my arms around her slouched shoulders and bear-hug her until her feet leave the ground.

"Nicholas was just like that," I say.

"Really?" she perks up. "How long did it last? I mean, like between months four and five?"

"I distinctly remember a turning point two weeks ago when I could put him down for a few minutes without him becoming frantic," I offer. "He just turned five months. I guess it all passes." I say this to reassure both of us.

I have met Donna before, talked with her a couple of times, and never saw the rose until now. Her defenses are down. There is no need to grandstand, no need to fight against her own vulnerability.

I feel as though someone has waved a wand of ether under my nose.

It's a shame that we lose our vulnerability once times get easier. We tend to layer it with so much defense that it gets buried. A rose under snow.

I haven't met many others like Donna at the pool. There are pool mothers with a look of flint in their eye, who are hell-bent on letting you know they have gone before you and can now comment freely, if recklessly. "I almost hemorrhaged in delivery!" "You're seven months? My sister *miscarried* at seven months!" "Say goodbye to your marriage!" "Sex? Ha ha ha ha!"

I want to stand on the lifeguard's chair and shout: "ISN'T THIS *HARD*! ISN'T THIS THE *HARDEST* DAMNED THING WE'VE EVER DONE! HAVE YOU EVER FELT SO MUCH LOVE AND TERROR IN YOUR LIFE? HOW DID OUR MOTHERS DO IT? HOW ARE WE EVER GOING TO GET THROUGH IT?"

Nobody seems to talk about this in truthful terms. Grandstanders compare because they secretly wonder if they're doing it right. Grandstanding is just a cover, a veil that disguises the vulnerability that we all have but that so many of us pretend we don't.

I look in my baby's eyes, and I see—I feel—his vulnerability, but I can never again have his innocence. And because of this, I realize every day that I have a choice: to live with that vulnerability or to lock it up. Pretending I never saw it, felt it, knew it. Pretending that all of this is easy. Pretending that his existence hasn't changed the very essence of my being. Pretending that he is one more thing I can "do," one more thing I have conquered, one more thing that doesn't threaten my defenses.

We ought to be congratulating each other. Instead, there is a nonchalance among us. A conspicuous absence of alliance. We walk right by each other at the pool, on the street, at the mall, at the office—babies on our hips, over our shoulders, asleep in strollers—exchanging a thin smile in passing, a silent and anonymous gesture of recognition.

CHAPTER SEVEN

Let the Baby Drive

he midday sun has slipped behind a patch of ashen cloud, and the air is moist with the anticipation of an afternoon downpour. We are hunkered down for the day. Nicholas begins to cry, his limbs stiffening despite my efforts to comfort him. I nurse him, and soon he's fast asleep. After ten minutes of strategic planning, I gingerly lay him down; then I tiptoe in exaggerated steps toward my pillow like I'm in a Road Runner cartoon with pizzicato violins plucking as I make my dastardly escape.

I can feel myself sinking, through bedsheets and feathers, past the mattress coils, into the floorboards. My bones ache. I feel immobilized with fatigue. Silence fills the room like vapor. Soon, all I can hear is the distant thump of my heart. Then, as sudden as a thunderclap in the middle of a brilliant summer morning, I am jolted awake by a piercing wail, the now familiar zero-to-sixty cry that races through my arteries like espresso. I fume at the edge of the bed with my eyelids sewn shut, my joints and jaws clenched. I open my eyes, and discover him on his knees kneading his face into the mattress. When I lift him up, he belches so hard I think the neighbor upstairs has moved a cabinet across the hardwood floor.

As a mother, I ought to have the courage of my convictions. But I have yet to nail down either the courage or the convictions with relative certainty. This, I'm beginning to see, does not necessarily have to do with my unflagging maternal self-doubt.

It's that I see all the "convenient" babies around me, slumbering peacefully in their strollers, their mothers wearing clean clothes and chewing gum and making plans for the weekend. What's more, strangers, friends, sometimes even relatives, feel inclined to warn me that I may spoil my baby.

I look up "spoil" in Webster's Dictionary.

> **spoil,** *to take away the pleasure from, to fail to make as good as possible, to damage or ruin, to impair, detract from, to injure (esp. a child or domestic animal) with respect to character during the formative period by overindulgence or too much leniency, to pamper and make much of, to become less good, valuable, enjoyable or useful . . .*

I think about indulgence and love. I wonder why we think there is such a thing as *too much* loving. I wonder why loving a baby gets mixed up with spoiling in the first place. And why are children and domestic animals in the same sentence?

The waiting room is crowded just before lunchtime, so I am sitting thigh to thigh with other mothers and their babies in the "well" section. To my left is a thirtyish mother and, asleep in the car seat next to her, her four-week-old baby girl swaddled in pink fleece.

"What's her name?" I ask.

"Arianna," she says. "And your son?"

"Nicholas."

We talk briefly about labor amnesia and sleep deprivation and the magic of breast milk.

"I just want to see the doctor and ask him if it's alright to let her cry," she explains. "I really don't want to, but I just want to know if I should."

She didn't want to ask the doctor whether there was thimerosol in the vaccines or what to do about persistent cradle cap. She wanted his advice on how to respond to her own child. She wanted the doctor to define the terms of her relationship: how *much* love and attention should I give my baby?

As I look at this lovely woman and her beautiful newborn daughter, I wonder why so many of us parents have lost trust in ourselves and our own intuition. We tune out our baby's voice to better hear our own; then we muffle our own voices to better hear those of others. We need doctors, to be sure. But why do we need to outsource our parenting to them?

Even the most responsible, educated, unbiased doctors still have their opinions about parenting, and parents always have choices. So to the new mother sitting in the waiting room with her four-week-old waiting to ask someone if it's alright to let her baby cry, I ask this: what do *you* think?

I'm trying so hard to think small, to stop seeing my baby as the tidal wave that threatens to drown me. But it's so hard to act contrary to our fears. And we are so fearful of losing control of ourselves, our sense of order and balance. As much as I want to see the situation from my baby's vantage point, when I feel compromised, jeopardized, utterly whipped with fatigue, all I hear is the sound of steel doors bolting shut within me. *Do you have to need me so much?*

Well, actually, yes.

Think small. I whisper it under my breath when my sciatic

nerve is throbbing down my leg. I repeat it like a yoga mantra.

Think small. Think small. Think small.

What is my son trying to tell me through his variety of cries, each one a different timbre, tone, pitch, and rhythm? Can I translate what he is saying, or do I only imagine his laundry list of baby grievances? Depends how tired I am.

"Don't let him run your life!" my neighbor Rob cautions.

I'm supposed to have a baby and arrange my life so that it doesn't look like I had one. The less reorganization of my life, the more it appears that I am managing. The more my present life resembles my former life, the more kudos I seem to get.

"He sure knows how to get what he *wa-a-ants!*" my girlfriend Amy chimes.

We think that if we teach the baby not to want, then the toddler won't want and the adult won't want because wanting is a terrible, terrible thing. Wanting is selfish. Greedy. Wanting invites disappointment because we don't always get what we want in life. We balk at the idea that a baby knows what he needs, because we assume that his needs will become his demands. We're afraid that might make him powerful. And we don't want powerful babies.

But, after just six months of motherhood, I can already see that a baby's wants and needs are pretty much one and the same. Twenty-four weeks out of the womb, my baby needs more than food, sleep, and a clean diaper. He wants—and *needs*—to be held, to bond for his healthy growth. By this time next year, I imagine he will *want* to eat an ice cream sandwich for breakfast. Play in the snow without shoes. Stand naked in the rain under the eaves trough with his mouth open. As his wants and needs begin to diverge, I will have to discern which ones are which, and respond to him accordingly, depending on the circumstances. Do we think that curbing a baby's wants and needs early on will prepare him for later? Or prepare *us* to set limits in toddlerhood when a growing child won't easily take no for an answer?

What does a baby ask of his mother? What is she willing to give?

What if a high-need baby has a mother who wants a low-maintenance child? What if a colicky baby's mother can't stand crying and cannot tolerate her own helplessness? What happens when a mother who is uncomfortable with neediness and dependency brings home a sensitive newborn who wants to be held a lot?

A child will adapt to suit his or her parent's needs, but at what cost?

I think about how need, love, and fear coexist. Who emerges from the complex process of sewing an abiding bond between mother and baby? How is each of us changed in the process?

I can see now why these first few years are so important, how they might set the stage for a person's whole approach to parenting. I realize how much is at stake, how invisible and crucial the stakes are.

I hear voices out there, a Greek chorus chanting at me to show him who's boss.

I do the only thing I can do under the circumstances: *I let the baby drive*. I let his cues guide me. I try to see his needs as worthy of my response. To imagine those needs as pressing and fleeting at the same time.

In letting the baby drive, I am not handing over the keys and the wheel. I let him navigate while I steer. In so doing, I discover what *drives* him. I am getting to know him, which offers me more than just personal information about my child—it gives me ideas about how to parent him.

It occurs to me that my perceptions of myself and of my child will determine my attitude toward him, my role as his mother, my behavior and his. What if some of those perceptions are negative? Or mistaken? Limited? False?

———

By the end of the day, my backbone is on fire, and my arms are numb. I want to bathe this boy and dress him for bed, but he won't lie still. It's like baby pro wrestling.

Here's where I make the leap. This is the pivotal point where I begin to perceive him as resistant. A twenty-eight-week-old hostile opponent. In my delirious fatigue, I assume that he's being uncooperative. It's dominoes from here on out. His squirming is his resistance is his rejection of me.

Being able to calm him consoles *me*. Not being able to calm him summons feelings of impotence and powerlessness in me. It smites me hard in the forehead: that's why I feel resentful. It's not that he's unhappy, like I initially thought when he was an inconsolable newborn; no, he's just uncomfortable. I can make a very short jump from his unhappiness to his dissatisfaction, and an even shorter one to his disapproval.

What if I allow these emotions to come between myself and my child? Wouldn't I then see his needs as insatiable demands and find it easier to deny him?

I love my baby, but can I also accept him when he is fussy, cranky, and unreceptive to my consolation? I have a sense that my difficulty in embracing these less desirable behaviors—even perceiving them as *less* desirable in the first place—would be a kind of rejection of him on some level. I notice that when I stop sniffing for his dissatisfaction, I can respond to him without fear. This clears the path for me to appreciate his unique needs, and parent him accordingly.

"You're just like my wife!" my friend Tony teases. "I tell her all the time, you don't have to meet *all* of the baby's needs!"

At six foot five, he towers over our conversation, gesturing to me in large circles.

"But which of my baby's needs should I respond to, and which ones should I dismiss? Do I quash one need and encourage another? And what would he do with the need that I ignored? Where would it go?" I spew.

"But if he gets *all* of his needs met, he'll end up thinking that he should get them all met later too!" Tony insists. "Once he's out in the real world, I bet he'll have a rude awakening!"

His arms are flapping so fast now he looks as if he's about to take flight.

"My baby has enough on his plate right now with gas alone," I say, deadpan. "Isn't gas enough of a rude awakening?"

We both explode with hysterical laughter.

Parenting is serious business, but once in a while, we need to make a wholehearted mockery of ourselves.

Over the last few months, I've watched the tension drain from my baby's face. His eyes have stopped darting, his furrowed brow has relaxed, his fists have released. He would come to the breast nearly frenzied. Now, he nurses with his arm resting across his forehead like he has had a long day. He thumps his chest, then mine. He Tarzan, me Jane.

At the dinner table, Dave and I pull his high chair up between us as the three of us discuss world events, politics, the economy. His arms flail with excitement, and he speaks in that dialect only babies can understand.

"Really?" we say. "Then when happened?"

His little body buckles with muted laughter, his mouth open to twice the size of anything else on his face.

"Ahhghzzch . . ." he says, grinning with a kind of baby bravado. He smiles, his chin glistening with drool, his two lone teeth jutting up from his pink gums, and I could swear he's saying, "Thanks . . . I feel better now."

CHAPTER EIGHT

Rising Son

riends who telephone after 7:30 p.m. snicker when I whisper hello.

"Baby sleeping?" they ask rhetorically.

They either (a) don't currently have a baby, (b) never had a baby, (c) don't want a baby, or (d) have a baby who could sleep undisrupted if you wheeled his bassinet onto the floor of the New York Stock Exchange when the Dow hit thirteen thousand. I've seen those babies. They're the ones napping in their car seats at a Bond movie.

"Your baby should get used to the noise," offers our childless friend Pam, who dropped in for a visit. "We had seven kids in the house growing up, and we just had to learn to sleep through it all."

"Some babies wake more easily," I retort defensively, recalling that since birth Nicholas could be stirred by a hushed conversation or a sneeze in the next room or the microwave that beeps three times when Dave's mug of coffee is ready.

But the conversation is already over. She leaves shaking her head, thinking that I am going about this sleep thing all wrong. I lock the door behind her thinking that she has a cat.

———

It isn't long before the mother of a "night-waker" begins to hear voices. Everyone weighs in with a suggestion, an explanation, a cure, and sometimes a warning. A doctor tells me that I'll train a "night-feeder" if I continue to nurse my baby at night.

"If you give a person chocolate cake every night, he will wake up for cake," he explains.

By the time I leave his office and lumber back to the car with my son, I feel like I am harboring a dark family secret. A *night-feeder*? Sounds like an earthworm, not a baby. Some kind of larval specimen found deep in the Amazon jungle. A bat foraging for food under a full moon. A mole digging up soil in search of its meal.

I want chocolate cake.

Standing in line at the supermarket, I am surrounded by glossy magazine covers promising me three steps to curing night-waking, six nighttime no-no's, eight surefire ways to get a baby to sleep the night. I flip to an article, and see a list of the do's and don'ts of sleep parenting.

In a small box titled Five Bedtime Sins, I read:

- Nursing baby to sleep
- Rocking baby to sleep . . .

Before I can read any further, the whole room seems to go white around me. I stare at the bedtime sin list. I do both of these, I think. Heck, sometimes simultaneously.

Suddenly, I am the only mother in the store, at the pool, in the country who is up at night. My eyes glaze over, and I think, well, there you have it: I'm a sinner. A bedtime sinner. I put the magazine back on the rack.

There are times when I feel so alone. It seems that every parent I talk to is enjoying the benefits of a Good Night's Sleep. No matter where I meet a perfect stranger with her baby, she pounces on the sleep issue within twenty seconds.

"She's a good sleeper."

"He sleeps so much, I have to wake him up to go to playgroup."

Most people think of night-waking as a calamity (which it can feel like after a while), but more than that, they see a baby's sleep pattern as the *mother's* fault.

I have become my boy's defense attorney. He lies there accused of deliberate night-waking and maternal manipulation, all before he can even speak. He'll become a great sleeper, I predict. I say this to myself often, and sometimes I really, really believe it.

Sometimes, he's so tired he is out in less than a minute. Sometimes, bedtime shifts from *Swan Lake* to *Riverdance*. I try to contain him, lulling, hushing, slowly lassoing his arms and legs one by one. When Nicholas is finally asleep, he is like an amusement park that has gone dark for the night.

I look for patterns. I keep sleep logs to see if I can find a rhythm to his sleep spurts. When he does sleep through the night, I find myself backtracking. What did he eat? How long did he nap, and how close to bedtime? Was it the garlic on my pasta? What did he wear to sleep—the outfit that snaps in the front or the back, the cotton or velour sleeper, the one with feet or without? For a while, I ascribe to the Evening Poop Theory, which has him sleeping soundly through the night after a monumental diaper just before bath and bedtime. Largely unfounded. We play with variables: Give him a later bath (too tired). Feed him an earlier dinner (hungry later on). Try oatmeal as filler (doesn't fill him). Dim the lights after dinner (he can see just as well in the dark). Play soft music (inspires him to sing).

At ten months, without warning and for no apparent reason, he begins to sleep eight hours at a stretch, which makes me want to dance naked in the living room without drawing the blinds.

Of course, the eight hours is not always of my choosing. He wakes one morning at 2:30 a.m., flapping his arms before takeoff. At 2:31 a.m., we have a sort of baby-parent summit meeting.

"Nicholas, when it's dark, people sleep, and they don't wake up until it's light out."

He puckers his lips and blows me a kiss. He can't understand the problem. He has just logged eight dreamy hours, and wants to announce it to every piece of living-room furniture. At 2:32 a.m., I explain to him that I am in need of rest in order to have the energy to take care of him. This fool's logic is met with a strange hissing that sounds like he has let the air out of a party balloon.

Another night, he goes down at 7:30 p.m. and wakes up eight hours later. I talk with him about rest and melatonin and the deterioration of brain cells due to lack of sleep in people past the age of thirty-five, but he is weepy and I am sleepy, and the bubbling lava of aggravation begins to erupt, rising from my chest to my throat. It hits me like a meteor crashing on our front porch: I am so tired of being tired, tired of his night-waking, tired of hearing how Bonnie's son has slept through the night since birth or how Lynn's daughter simply has to be laid down in her crib awake to put herself to sleep.

In a firm and gentle voice, I tell Nicholas that I want him to settle back down and Go To Sleep. Then I stagger to my mattress a scant seven feet away. Inside of two seconds, he stands with his hands on the railing of his crib and begins to cry intensely. I get up again and stand with my head on the door frame, staring at the small lit numbers on the thermostat for twenty-five more seconds. When I pick him up, he grabs my pajama sleeve and won't let go. So I bring him to bed with me.

At 3:35 a.m., tucked between Dave and me, Nicholas falls asleep on his left side (for twenty minutes), then flips to his right side (for another twenty minutes), then does a somersault onto his belly, then a cartwheel, landing on his back, where he snoozes for another half-hour. Somewhere between the somersault and the cartwheel, I finally manage to doze off. Suddenly, during one of his gymnastic dismounts, Nicholas thwacks me in the left eye with a baby fist.

I lie there in a groggy stupor, with my palm over my eye, listening to my son snore, with the corner of the nightstand in the small of my back.

"We have to do something," Dave blurts in the dead of night. "This can't go on."

Despair seems to dissipate at dawn. Everything feels different when shame and anger and fear and the love of convenience aren't rolling dice after midnight.

People look at me with a mix of sympathy and suspicion when they hear that my baby wakes up at night. As if his sleep patterns are a product of *my* inability to teach him to sleep on his own.

The magazines and books and neighbors and pool mothers and cashiers and bank tellers and taxi drivers insist that I simply ignore him and go back to bed. (And these are the people I didn't ask.) What would they say if I were talking about an elderly person? Or a beloved family dog?

Parents seem to pitch their tents in one of two campgrounds: Camp Cry-It-Out, where night-waking babies cry alone in the dark until they learn to sleep through the night, or Camp Pick-Me-Up, where night-waking babies are picked up and soothed in the dark until they learn to sleep through the night.

I know a lot of people who have pitched their tents in Camp Cry-It-Out. One couple sat in their bedroom while their eight-month-old son wailed in the dark for a half hour in his crib. They sat next to each other on the edge of their bed with their fingernails in their teeth, kicking the bed rails. After a half hour, the crying stopped. They walked into their baby's room and found him asleep on his knees, his little head leaning against the two crib slats his fingers were still clutching. The sight of him was enough to make them pull up their tent pegs and march across to the other campsite.

I know another mother who let her six-month-old son cry it out while she lay down on the floor next to his crib so he couldn't see her, "just to make sure he was okay." And another woman I know refused to even go into her daughter's room because she was annoyed that the nine-month-old girl was "only crying to get my attention."

An acquaintance who describes herself as a "militant Ferber-izer" in the early months of her daughter's life now laments that, nearly four years later, her preschooler is "the world's worst sleeper, up at the crack of dawn and cranky until way past dinner," at which point their home becomes a bedtime battleground for several more hours.

There are those people who spook mothers about picking up the crying, night-waking baby, warning them that it will only encourage him to keep waking up. Personally, I have found the exact opposite to be true. Somehow, the more I pick up my baby when he cries, it seems the *less* he cries. Now he may wake up during the night, roll over, and go back to sleep.

Forcing a baby to cry out his discomfort or anxiety *looks* like it works, because the baby does eventually stop crying. But does it teach him to sleep because it's time for bed, or does it teach him to sleep because nobody's coming?

I know it can be inconvenient to live by the baby's schedule. But I just don't believe that this baby who is afraid of vacuums and Velcro is deliberately trying to wreck my night.

Every baby has his list of reasons for night-waking. My son is no exception. I can now add broccoli to that list.

One night, he wakes up at 3 a.m., terribly upset. I find him sitting up looking frightened and confused. When I ask him what is wrong, he glances up at me in tears and says, "Ba-ca-ba."

Translation: broccoli.

I hold him until his sobs subside. I keep thinking, He was awakened by *broccoli*. Was it a head? A floret? He doesn't elaborate.

Veggie nightmares notwithstanding, nobody likes being interrupted from a good night's sleep. So a baby who wakes his parents up after midnight may be misperceived as controlling—controlling the amount of rest we get, controlling the way we feel physically and emotionally, threatening our sense of well-being, our sex life, our marriage, our work, our finances—which can cast everything in another light entirely.

Chronic lack of sleep, for the record, is a nasty little exercise in self-erosion. It is no wonder that sleep deprivation is considered a form of torture for prisoners of war. It's easy to see how four or five nights of inconsolable crying can be easily rationalized by Camp Cry-It-Out parents. Any guilt is assuaged by scores of people who not only assure parents that crying it out is not harmful to an infant, but suggest that it's the only way to "break a bad habit" or avert a full-blown "sleep problem." Nobody likes those words. Habit. Problem. So parents can let a baby scream into the dark night because they think it's better for everyone in the long run.

On the other hand, there are parents, pediatricians, and psychologists who believe that while a baby won't die from crying it out, he can nonetheless shut down in some way that may not be immediately evident, interfering with his internal sense of security and trust in his caretakers. Who is to say that such distress and frustration do not plant the seeds of anxiety, mistrust, and self-doubt in an infant, seeds that take root in him and grow?

How we handle night-waking depends on who we consult, whether we are fond of stats and studies to support or contradict our beliefs, which books we choose to read, what kind of family baggage we carry into parenthood, and what our baby's needs trigger in us.

In other words, it depends on what we want to believe.

One fact clearly emerges: sleeping the night is a very touchy subject for parents. It's way up there with whether to spank, whether mothers should work full-time outside the house. It's as divisive a topic as gun control, abortion, or nuclear disarmament.

Cry-It-Out versus Pick-Me-Up. These are two entirely different sensibilities. And both camps are vehement about their choices. A woman I know lost a longtime friend because this friend and her husband moved their two-year-old daughter from her crib to a bed and then tied the door handles to the wall so she couldn't come out of her room during the night. Those parents felt their daughter had to learn, even as a toddler, that Mommy and Daddy aren't always there. My friend, on the other hand, couldn't bear to listen to stories of how the little girl screamed in terror for her mother in the dark from behind the locked door. After twenty years of shared views, the two friends called it a night. Permanently.

Pick-Me-Up points a finger across the divide at Neglect, and Cry-It-Out shakes her head at Indulgence. It's partisan politics. Neither group is at all inclined to see issues from the other party's perspective. Unfortunately, in the parenting arena, there is a child in the middle.

After months of erratic night-waking, I can personally declare that the sleep thing is now pretty much a nonissue. Between his eighth tooth and the appearance of his first molar, Nicholas has suddenly begun to sleep from dark to light. I am Julie Andrews in *The Sound of Music,* yodeling on a pastoral hillside.

I certainly haven't enjoyed my son's night-waking. Many times, I feel as though I have suffered it. On not a few occasions, I have felt twitches of doubt, resentment, shame.

Nursing my baby whenever he has woken up crying hasn't trained a night-feeder after all—it has trained a communicator. Picking him up and rocking him back to comfort hasn't taught him to need my help going to sleep—instead, it seems to have taught him to need my help when he's in pain, to feel secure in the knowledge that he is not alone. And, somehow, when he's not awakened by sore gums or a stomach cramp or a giant broccoli, it has trained a sleeper.

CHAPTER NINE

Just Call Me Daddy

here's nothing quite like that period of time between the baby's first vowels and the moment you actually hear your name come out of his tiny mouth.

You lie awake in your bed at the break of day, your eyelids still sewn together, and you listen to the symphony of sounds:

"Aaa-eee. Baaa-yeee. Daa-daa-daa."

Your feet feel like they're being tickled with peacock feathers.

The vocabulary comes overnight. One day, the baby is gurgling; the next, he's reciting *Macbeth*. "They had more in them than mortal knowledge." That's how a proud parent hears it.

Listen, he said, "Coquilles Saint-Jacques." I swear. Wait, he just said, "Margaret Thatcher"; no, it was "thatched hut." And he hasn't even said "kitty cat" yet.

The kid's a freaking genius.

Our boy Nicholas, approaching one year points to the "windoo" and tells me the "lahn-moa" woke him up from a nap. He sets his own menu: "towst, cheeez, noo-dow, chik-in." Knows when it's time for his "bass," when he's ready to go to "seep." Greets people and inanimate objects with a lilting "hi-yee!" then an interrogative "buh-bye?"

He can say Mah. As in "mahn-go."

He can say Mee. As in "mee-ow."

But he doesn't say Mah-mee.

As in me.

Do I mind that he knows how to form the *plural,* for crying out loud, but can't squeeze a singular "Mommy" in there for the heck of it? Does it bother me? Do I worry that there is absolutely no sign of "Mommy" amid his numerous soliloquies, dramatic readings, and comic improv?

"Dah-deeeeee!"

Dave stands in the front hallway by the door, and Nicholas speed-waddles over to him with arms extended. We think it's adorable beyond all reckoning. So does Larry the mailman, whom Nicholas also greets in the same way. And José, the butcher at the supermarket down the road. And me.

"Dah-dee!" says Nicholas the moment he catches a glimpse of me in the morning. He stands in his crib, his puffy knuckles on the white railing, his eyes never leaving my face. The meaning of life is in his gaze. That smile, those pomegranate cheeks flushed a deep pink like he's been tobogganing all day, that soft crackly morning voice and those temples creased from bedsheets.

I feel like he has known me my whole life.

My mother suggests that once he finds his *m*, he'll be onto "Mommy" in no time. Thanks, but he found his *m* in the cow jumped over the "m-m-m-moooon." And he moos with great conviction.

People have found it odd.

"Really?" a friend queried. "My baby said 'mama' right off the bat. In fact, that was her first word."

And they look at me and then my baby, and say, "I guess you're *Daddy's* little guy, eh?" Like I am the live-in nanny. As if maybe the kid is confused, you know, not too bright.

"Good morning, sweetheart!" I coo.

"Dah-dee!" he blurts.

"Baby, it's Mommy. *Mah-mee*," I correct gently.

"Dah-dee," he insists, like I've got it wrong.

"Mommy," I volley back.

"Mango," he retorts matter-of-factly, changing the subject entirely.

I sit in front of him, imagining myself celebrating Father's Day alongside Dave, both of us holding cards from our son. Will he ever say it?

I feel a hot flash of mistaken identity.

I had thought about what it might be like to be a mother, but I never imagined what it might feel like to be called Mommy. I never expected one little word to send me into a tailspin of self-doubt and redefinition.

One morning, at precisely nine minutes past six, I walk to Nicholas in his crib, and there he is grinning at me like he just reeled in the Big One.

"Mah-mee," he states for the record. The accent on the first syllable, the pitch high-low, the eyes fixed, inquisitive, knowing. In case I am imagining things, he says it again. The word is drenched in one hundred percent pure maple syrup. It's smooth and lush. I feel it rush through my veins, pulsing down my arms to my fingertips, racing down my legs and back up my spine where it pools warmly in my ears.

He calls me Mommy. He *identifies* me.

Soon, I hear him call me, greet me, mumble the word in passing, beckon me, cry out for me, acknowledge me. There's the standard Mommy "Hi, how are ya" greeting. There's the one that sounds like the bing-bong of a doorbell. He says it when he plays in pillows, on the living-room floor, his tiny face burrowed in tassels and fringes, rolling from side to side doing the front crawl and coming up for air.

He says it quenchingly when I slice squares of orange, cantaloupe, and pear and place them on his tray. He says it under his breath when he is chewing them, and the juice gushes over his lips. He says it when I wrap him in a towel after the bath that leaves his toes pruny. "Co-zee," he whispers softly as I hug him in terry cloth.

"Mah-mee." He holds the vowels. "Maaaah-meeee."

He says the word like it's steeped in gratitude. Sometimes, there is an aw-shucks quality to it. Other times, he says it with the solemnity of a praying monk. Sometimes, he says it in a half whisper, without even looking at me. He smiles and stares off into the distance, as if he's flirting with a recollection. Sometimes, he bellows it as though he's doing play-by-play at the Super Bowl.

Nicholas now stares deep into his father's eyes and blurts "Mah-mee" without blinking; then he zips right past him on his way down the forty-yard line. I look at Dave apologetically.

"Don't take it personally, honey," I reassure him. "It's just a phase."

The tables have turned. Only now, Dave isn't Mommy. He isn't Daddy either. He is, as he likes to refer to himself these days, "Chopped Liver."

He walks in the door at the dinner hour, and announces his arrival with his arms in the air like a referee.

"Nicholas! Chopped Liver is home! Whoo-*hoo*!"

The baby looks up at him, smiles, and mumbles. "Mah-mee," and then resumes his activity. Dave sighs heavily, tosses the mail on the piano, and trudges down the hall to the walk-in closet where I presume he feels inclined to live temporarily.

I had heard that babies can prefer one parent over another at certain times, and may alternate doing so as a normal part of development. Nothing personal. Or permanent. Nevertheless, I try to compensate.

"Mah-mee!" the boy croons rapturously.

"Hi honey! And he-e-e-e-ere's *Daddy*!" I lob back.

"Mah-mee," he retorts, staying on message.

"S'awright," murmurs Dave.

Sigh. I feel like Mother Earth, and Dave feels like a compost heap.

With "Dah-dee" briefly out of favor, I am now on call 24-7. At this particular moment in time, I am the Chosen One. Dave curls up to read with our baby, hold him, whisper in his ear, but his little arms elbow Dave in the sternum, trying to break free of his father's loving embrace.

"Mah-mee! Mah-mee!"

Sometimes, I wrestle with the great need demons when I have no energy, when I need momentary relief from my Mommy moniker. My name seems lost in the ether. My role rules. I am the catch of the day. I begin to feel the netting over me, and I want to duck and roll in the fetal position, fighting to free myself yet pulling the mesh blanket around me.

I am consciously ignoring the mountain of clothes on our bed and the kitchen sink so full of dishes and cutlery you'd think we catered a block party. I chew a forkful of dinner.

"Mah-mee? Mah-mee!"

I try not to get up and walk over to my husband and baby, try not to forfeit my meal so that Mommy can take over from Daddy, who is perfectly capable. I chew, while Dave, growing frustrated and weary, occasionally glances at me like this may not be a phase at all but a permanent way of life.

I lie in bed at 6:30 a.m. with an extra hour of shut-eye ahead of me. Dave takes Nicholas, and through the haze of half sleep, I can hear them reading, playing, talking in the room down the hall. I listen as Dave pulls open wooden drawers looking for Nicholas's clothes, slides the closet doors open, and tries to dress him for their morning stroll. The baby begins to fuss and cry, while Dave tries to pull a shirt over his head.

I fidget, turn, and rearrange my pillow. I want to tell Dave to stretch the shirt a little before putting it on Nicholas's head, to pull it over from the crown of his head first to make it easier. I try to shake it off, but I can hear the faint click of breakfast spoons on glass bowls and I want to mention that the baby's oatmeal is in the fridge. At the back. On the first shelf. I want to remind him about the Tri-Vi-Flor vitamins.

I lift my head, whack my pillow in the middle with my fist to change its shape, and slam my head into the center of it. I hear Dave changing a diaper while the baby squirms and cries, and I want to tip him off about doing trumpet sounds with his mouth to the tune of "Old MacDonald."

I can't drown out the activity outside the bedroom door any more than I can tune out the noise in my own head. Here I am, lying under warm covers, my eyes closed, having an imaginary conversation with my husband, berating myself for squandering my one hour of bonus sleep to parent from my pillow.

Mommy is larger than life. Bigger than oatmeal and matching socks. Who am I? I am Mother. Mama. Soothsayer. I am the comfort zone. The safety net. The nurturer. Relief, reassurance, warm arms, a tall drink of water. But where did *I* go—the I that is within me regardless of circumstance and blood relations?

I have become the star of my baby's show, standing center stage, but just for one fleeting moment, I want to duck into the dark side wings and disappear into the shadows. I want to let my consciousness burble like a mountain stream, trickle down, down, down the shores of my mind, to the place where thoughts go when they have been allowed to run their course. The thought pool at the mouth of the river, just before it joins the sea of Big Ideas. Where could it go from there? Where could *I* go?

"Mommy." I love hearing the word. It grounds me. It gives me the most sublime pleasure to hear it slip from my boy's lips and fill the stale air with magic.

And sometimes, when I am unsure that I'm able to live up to his expectations or mine, it makes me feel cornered, hot, weepy, in a room with no doors or windows. Sometimes, I want to sit and do nothing. Mommy's tired. Mommy is having a bite to eat. Mommy needs to rest for a few minutes. Mommy is fading like a ham radio signal.

"*Mommy, Mommy, Mommy.*"

I'm . . . right . . . here.

Mommy's here.

Mommy's always here.

CHAPTER TEN

The Pact

y son and I begin walking our second lap around the block on a misty afternoon, when we approach a small traffic jam by the stone house on the corner. A dozen or so cars are jockeying for position along this otherwise sleepy suburban cul-de-sac, parking illegally, leaving tire tracks on the neighbors' lawns. Two yellow balloons are tied to the black antique lamppost by the front entrance. People are swarming the path to the porch, walking hastily past two neat piles of cut firewood on either side of the door, squeezing past people coming out of the house and down the front steps. A small sign under the balloons invites us all in for an open house.

Nicholas is strapped into my kangaroo pouch, facing outward. The front hall echoes with the sound of heels on oak floors and a low-grade murmur of people moving in and out of the vestibule. The living room is taped off like the scene of a crime. Perfect strangers are rifling through books and knickknacks, kitchen appliances and Christmas decorations, like civil looters sifting politely through wreckage for something shiny and interesting.

I overhear two women whispering about how the couple got divorced and sold the house, about how he had someone else, how she took their three kids and left.

We shuffle slowly across hardwood floors, eavesdropping, walking among the ruins of another family's life. My baby's head bobs under my chin as we gaze at floral walls papered in Laura Ashley, and I tiptoe into the kitchen with the breakfast nook and the generous bay window where the built-in bench is now covered with old books. *Resurrection* by Tolstoy, one dollar. *The Joy of Sex,* fifty cents. Cookie cutters in the shape of Santa Claus, twenty-five cents. Wineglasses, four for a dollar. A dusty DustBuster. A coffeemaker. Flower baskets. Dried roses. Snow boots. A computer printer. A plaid umbrella with a wooden handle.

Images of a broken home. Portrait of a broken pact.

I stare out the kitchen window at an abandoned swing set on a straw patch of grass in a barren backyard. My eyes sting as my vision grows hazy. I daydream through the back alleys of my marriage long before my husband and I even conceived of conceiving. We once talked about big-picture subjects: philosophy, art, the origin of religions, psychology, travel, literature. Now and apparently unflinchingly, we can discuss our son's bowel movements while dining on a succulent beef stew. We get really excited about a good poopy diaper. I mean, *really* excited.

Things have changed. And it's not just the conversation.

Years ago, during hypothetical chats about parenthood, Dave and I made an agreement. Nothing formal. We affectionately called it The Pact. Simply put, I would get up with our baby, and Dave would sleep. *I* actually came up with this quaint plan. The man has to make sense by day, I reasoned, string together complete sentences, sound coherent with other adults. At that particular juncture in my life, I thought, I will stay home with our baby. I could wear pajamas all day without threat of termination. The neighbors wouldn't necessarily have to know I slept in those sweatpants.

In practice, The Pact is a masterpiece when our baby boy sleeps through the night. When he doesn't, The Pact is the worst screwball idea I ever conjured up.

Fatigue has a way of making everything come to the surface. It makes things look bigger than they really are, like objects in your side-view mirror. It makes otherwise sensible people feel raw and exposed, threatened and defended.

Dave says that it reminds him of his days on the front lines in Vietnam when he was forced to go weeks without sleep. I remind him that he has never, in fact, been to Vietnam. He admits that sleep deprivation has taken its toll on him as well.

I had always wondered how on earth couples could have a baby and not spend the rest of their days stoned on bliss. I never understood how—after a symbiotic embrace with their newborn—people could even entertain the notion of growing apart.

Now I see how a person can become too tired to talk, too tired to care if the last misunderstanding was sorted out, if the last disappointment was aired or swallowed. Until it gets lodged in your throat and you can't breathe anymore. You lose interest in who had the first or last word. Words take energy. Thinking before you blurt. Choosing the right phrases. Hearing the right message. Building bridges takes energy. Crossing them is a whole other story.

Part of the difficulty lies not simply in the baby's night-waking, but in the curious and unmistakable differences between mothers and fathers.

In the middle of a perfectly silent night, Nicholas coughs like a cat trying to expel a hairball, and I'm doing my best Dick Van Dyke flip off the mattress and over the ottoman while Dave mumbles, "Should we check on him, hon?"

Don't get me wrong. My husband is a good man. Where most men would kill for a trip to the moon, he'd love to have a womb for a day. In labor. (I added that last part.) He was awestruck during my entire pregnancy, talking into my navel daily, "reporting live" as if it were a fetal microphone.

Now, for the first time in our relationship, we are playing roles that we cannot easily interchange. Our roles are partly assigned by nature, partly assumed by our own natures, and partly due to the effects of the postpartum pendulum swinging to the extremes until we find a balance.

Until we find a balance.

Is this even possible? No matter how much a father cherishes his child, there still exists a separateness between them. No matter how much Dave adores our son, his breasts have never leaked when he cries.

It already seems like a lifetime ago that we were lying side by side on our mattress in the dark doing a sort of belly Braille, running our four hands over the Great Bump in search of tiny elbows, knees, heels. The night was filled with a whispery laughter, the kind that knows something wonderful is just around the corner. The baby was still an abstraction. A mystery person. A name with no voice.

Bump had not yet stirred an intoxicating brew of mixed emotions in his father for taking up so much of Mom's time, energy, and attention. The baby had not yet awakened in his mother the breathtaking despair of round-the-clock caretaking that can make a person want to leap at the first chance to walk grocery aisles alone after dark.

My friend Janet says that after their baby was born, her husband became the observer, the outsider looking in, and then began to resent being left out.

"Then *I* started to resent *him* for feeling resentful," she recalls. "How dare you? I thought. Stop being a big baby! I have a *baby*. Can't you understand that?"

Since the birth of their daughter, Janet admits she feels disoriented, frustrated that her husband knows what time it is, what day it is, what he ate for breakfast. He can sleep soundly through the baby's gurgles, cries, and feedings, through his wife's postmidnight activity.

"So wake me up!" he insists, knowing that she won't because, when sleep-deprived, he's inclined to leave the gas stove on simmer and the baby's bottle in the cupboard next to the cayenne pepper.

In the morning, he yawns and moans that he's exhausted, and she rolls her eyes into the back of her head.

AnnDee remembers how she would tend to her colicky baby all day, and then hand him to her husband the moment he walked in the front door.

"It's your turn," she'd say in desperation, while he stared at her with injured eyes. "He was fantasizing about this loving greeting, this warm welcome, this playful environment with a sexy wife and an adorable baby. He didn't want to feel like the boy in his mother's house. His life seemed unmoved by the birth of our child, whereas mine was completely overturned."

And Melina recalls how her husband Richard would come home from work and greet his baby daughter with a round of woodpecker kisses and peekaboo before he even said hello to his wife.

"He'd coo and gurgle at her, flashing big smiles, then turn to me and change gears completely. It's like he could muster all the energy in the world for her, but when it came to me, it was, 'So how're you doing?' I felt like a piece of furniture," she says.

"I just remember walking up our driveway to the front door bracing myself," Richard recalls. "I would leave her alone all day with the baby. It's as if I didn't want to know just how she was feeling because I didn't want to feel guilty. The sad thing is, we never talked about it, and that has hurt us over the years."

Expecting our first baby, did we ever imagine that this triangle of our new family could prick us with its sharp edges?

———

I can't sleep. The blurry red numbers on the clock say 3:04 a.m. Nicholas is in dreamland. Dave is out cold on his back with his arms over his head and the covers at the foot of the bed. It's so quiet I think I can hear my eyes blinking.

I wonder how it happened. The couple in the stone house on the corner probably started out like most of us. How did they get from the altar to the delivery room to the open house selling off their Santa Claus cookie cutters?

People had told me life was going to change. Maybe *this* is that life. That change. Is it that our lives have changed, or have *we* changed? Is this a matter of changing circumstances, or has the baby's presence created in us, between us, a permanent shift in our sensibilities, our needs, our self-perceptions, our sexuality, our posture, gait, breathing?

Sometimes, I can feel the thick vines of disillusionment reaching around me, twisting around my sweatpants spotted with baby cereal, around my hair that I haven't had a minute or the desire to wash in three days, coiling around my chafed knuckles and skin breakouts and stiff muscles and lopsided breasts deflated and rearranged by breastfeeding. I can feel my self-esteem deflating too, like a slow leak from a tire.

"Keep the romance alive by setting aside one night of the week for a date," prescribes the relationship expert on a morning talk show I succumb to watching in my bone-tired stupor while my boy naps.

A *date?*

I guess I missed the segment where they mention the bit about how a baby's needs and helplessness can dredge up every parent's own unresolved childhood longings. Or the sidebar about how a baby holds a magnifying glass over a marriage, making otherwise invisible fissures and flaws plain as day to the naked eye.

It's easier to talk about aromatic bath oils, candles, and lace than it is to publicly discuss the ways in which tiny unspoken disappointments between spouses can fester into gaping wounds with only our most indestructible emotional defenses to cauterize them.

And we'll be back in just a moment. Stay with us . . .

Cue the music.

Dave must feel that I'm a tired new mother with nothing left for him. And I feel that I'm a tired new mother with nothing left for me.

"There's a hierarchy of needs," says AnnDee. "When a mother has a free moment, she wants to rest, be alone, do things for herself. But her partner wants her to give that free moment to him. Dad feels Mom and baby have an exclusive bond. Dad wants advice about baby, but he doesn't want Mom to tell him what to do. It's a power struggle. But more than that, it's a power *structure*."

It can become a test of wills. Who will submit? Will he? Will she? And the baby?

At a crowded picnic area by the river, a couple and their daughter are playing ball when the four-year-old runs precariously close to the water. The mother shrieks and lunges forward to grab her child.

"Relax! *Relax!*" her husband barks, grimacing at his wife as if a woman is supposed to react gracefully, tidily, attractively in an emergency. She looks as childlike as the little girl she just saved, only nobody jumps in to rescue the big girl from public ridicule.

He makes a scene about her making a scene.

What he's really saying is, Alright, I wasn't paying attention, but I'm not going to let you point it out to me. You think I'm an inadequate parent? Inferior? I'll show you . . . by making you feel inadequate and inferior instead.

Relax, relax.

Foreplay anyone?

Partners who are focused on protecting themselves from censure are not usually in the mood for love. Neither are those who are still expecting even *after* the baby is born.

My friend Jaqueline recalls that her ex-husband wanted her to be who she was before she became a mother.

"When you are grappling with sleep deprivation and your postpartum body, you feel very vulnerable," she says. "Self-judgment complicates everything."

It's not that a new mother doesn't want to be intimate with her husband after baby. It's just that sometimes a simple pat on the back can get the embers burning. I can remember exactly where I was and what I was wearing the day Dave said to me as I was changing the baby's clothes, "You're so good with him, honey." I could have jumped him right there, but I was too tired. (Still, the point is, I *wanted* to.)

Hello, my name is Lu. I have become a mother and an approval junkie. Am I coming across okay? Doing a good job? Just good? Not great? Doing the best job? You don't think I can do it all? Hey, who do you think I am, Superwoman? Do you still find me smart, beautiful, desirable, exciting? What was that look? Why don't you look at me that way anymore? You think after a twenty-eight-hour day of a baby attached to my body for food, comfort, and sleep, I want to have anyone *touch* me? Why won't you touch me anymore? Aren't I attractive to you? Why didn't you ask me about *my* day? Gee, what do you *think* I did today, market analysis? Don't you think I know what the baby needs since I'm *with* him all day? You're his *father,* what do *you* think he needs?

What is astounding to me is not that we feel these contradictions or that we direct them at our partner. But rather how we can say all of this without actually saying a word of it.

———

It's early evening. I have spent another day deeply engrossed in the minutiae of caretaking. Dave arrives, drained from another bustling day in Manhattan, where just getting through subway turnstiles requires his full vigilance and attention. I feel as though I have been walking in the desert for three days and he is the lemonade stand.

Before he puts down his briefcase and blueprints, I begin to share my shrewd and revelatory insights: what the baby's half cry/half chuckle means, how to get him into the high chair by putting three clean baby-jar lids or small plastic measuring cups on his tray, how his occasional fussing before or during his meal does not necessarily mean he isn't hungry but that he may want an ounce of water or maybe a Tupperware lid to chew on between bites, how to distract him with the box of Q-tips or bubbles or a slow animated version of "Sing a Song" long enough to change his diaper without him flipping off the changing table, how to coax his arms through his pajama sleeves by reciting entire stanzas from *Great Day for Up* from memory in falsetto.

I realize this may not be the best bit of timing. But somehow, I seem to have misplaced my ability to wait for the appropriate moment. I suppose I've been so overwhelmed by self-doubt and the intensity of our baby's needs that it feels a little heady to have figured out anything at all that actually works. So now that I have achieved a kind of routine with Nicholas, I feel oddly responsible for keeping it intact. This, of course, presumes that my way is the only way.

I seesaw dinner dishes under warm tap water in the kitchen sink while Dave prepares the baby's bath down the hall. I am free to retreat to another room in the house and curl up with one of the four novels I never have time to read. I can go for a walk or sit on the porch and take in the sunset. But I feel the lure of wet tiles, not to check on my husband while he bathes our son, but rather to, well, check *in*. The subtle distinction is lost on Dave.

"Did you test the water?" I ask with quiet urgency.

Dave turns his head toward me in slow motion, blinks once with feeling, then glares. I can see how a wife giving baby instructions to a husband can make him feel that she is not just the baby's mother, but his too.

"You don't trust me," he blurts under his breath.

"Of course I do. It's just that I do this all day, and uh . . ." I fumble, not sure where I'm going with this, but feeling pretty sure that I'm running the wrong way with the ball.

"This is not about trust," I insist. "And it's not about you."

It's difficult to separate our own beliefs from the messages we imbibed growing up. Whenever we heard of a tragedy involving a child, people's immediate response was, "Oh my God, and where was the *mother*?"

Women feel responsible. For everything. We also think that we do it better. And sometimes, we do. But is this about our performance—whether or not we can accomplish good parenting? Or is it about what we are willing to give in a relationship without keeping a tally? After the birth of a baby, somehow we don't perceive ourselves as equals with our spouses anymore.

We occasionally find ourselves working at cross-purposes. I calm our son down before bedtime, playing soft music, reading him quiet stories, lulling him into a baby zen state. Then Dave comes in for the hand-off, and twenty minutes later I hear a distinct whinnying coming from behind the door. Yes, they're playing pony.

My friend Tina says, "My husband gets our daughter all worked up just before bedtime, and then he can't calm her down."

So what happens?

"He passes the baby back to me, of course. So that I can calm her down—*again*. I'm thinking, Sure, you have fun with her, and then give *me* the challenge of trying to get a screaming, overtired ten-month-old to sleep. Gee, thanks." In the end, she admits that she'd just rather do it herself.

But mothering is not a call to omnipotence. If I feel like baby's sole caretaker simply because I spend more hours of the day with him, then I'm secretly going to believe that nobody can parent him as well as me.

And sometimes, it's not so secret.

The truth is that Daddy is entitled to figure out his own viable method. Just as a new mother needs to figure things out for herself, so does a new father. My brother-in-law, Michael, calls it "the pride of craftsmanship."

Dave is no slouch. The man can draw a three-dimensional axonometric picture of a building on a restaurant napkin with my eyeliner. He's a creative wizard. When he proposed, he put my engagement ring inside a hollowed-out egg that he had previously scored with an exacto knife, cleaned, and stuffed with a swatch of blue velvet material in which he poised the ring—and then served it to me for breakfast along with a half of a grapefruit and a toasted bagel. In other words, he is an idea guy who comes up with some pretty ingenious solutions.

So does it realy *matter* if Dave dilutes the baby's juice with two instead of three ounces of water? Does it truly make a difference whether he puts him in the snap-up pajamas or the zippered ones?

It's hard to let go. Not just of maternal guilt, but of roles and rules, perceptions, blueprints of family histories, the need for control, and a morbid fear of losing everything.

Lines blur. Lives blur. Unwittingly, I have begun to think and feel like a needed person. As if that's my new role and my new identity. It isn't a huge leap from here to the void, the black hole that sucks us in after we've lost our footing, our focus, ourselves. Not to mention our sense of humor.

Somewhere between the hospital parking lot and home, we forget how to have fun. Maybe that's because bringing a baby home to live with us can often feel more like crisis management than a honeymoon.

My pal Maria can remember how she'd call her husband Matt at work at the height of their baby's hysteria just so he could know what she was going through. She wanted empathy, not dinner and a movie.

Perhaps the success or failure of our pacts depends in large part on how we fare under stress. Having a baby is an unfathomable miracle that just so happens to scare the living daylights out of us.

How do fears and needs play out between parents? Do we panic and blame each other? Do we offer mutual support? Does one of us withdraw while the other takes over? Do we laugh? Cry? Hurl flatware? Or do we take the phone off the hook and get naked? (And if, perchance, we do get naked, do we discuss the baby's dinner menu, mortgage payments, strategies for averting tantrums? Do we jump with every peep of the baby monitor? How *present* do we allow ourselves to be?)

I suppose the question is not whether we are deeply invested or involved in child-rearing. If our commitment to parenthood was the issue, our pacts would probably hold up pretty well.

Clearly, mothers and fathers don't experience parenthood through the same lens. Not that we should or even can. That said, we might make a habit of exchanging lenses, of respecting each other's vision, if we are ever going to find a way to share one.

But what happens when each of us wants support and validation from the other at the very same time that we feel rejected by one another?

Stalemate.

Here is our first major hurdle as new parents. Some people make the leap, some never get over it, and some walk around it in opposite directions. This is the point that many couples may forget about over time, but never quite forgive.

As AnnDee avows, "There will always be this underlying conflict down the road, because we never addressed it at the beginning."

But how much of that conflict lives within each of us, regardless of marriage and children?

Standing in the sun-drenched kitchen of the broken home with the custom drapery and crown moldings, I pick up a creased paperback from the breakfast-nook bench and flip through its yellowed pages. *You Can't Go Home Again* by Thomas Wolfe, one dollar.

CHAPTER ELEVEN

The Thirty-Nine-Hour Errand

'm leaving tomorrow. It's going to be my first night away, alone, in my son's whole eleven-month life, and I have no conceivable idea how I will board a plane in New York, press my face against the window, and catch a glimpse of our house below until it becomes a tiny dot on the landscape. I feel like I am leaving a lung behind. Perhaps this is understating it too much.

Maybe Nicholas senses that his mother won't get much sleep tonight anyway, so he figures he'll keep me company. The night before my very first trip away from my baby, he is up every hour and a half.

He snores in my arms as I stare at his tiny parted lips. We sit in the rocker, and I gaze at his lovely face and feel his peace. I watch him through half-slit eyes while his mouth twitches with sleep grins, and think nothing in the world could be as good as this. Then, the chaos jolts me like an electric prod. My anxiety feels hot and itchy.

Barring any unexpected snowstorms and plane delays, I will be gone a total of thirty-nine hours. Maybe it will be like running a very long errand. A day and a half at the supermarket. Maybe Nicholas won't even notice the time, won't feel confused and disturbed by my absence, abandoned, too anxious to sleep or eat.

In fact, the more I imagine his eyes darting around the room in search of me, the more I want to cancel the trip. But I have already accepted the job. A one-day event—a Christmas parade, televised live on the USA network. I have been hired as a reporter to do off-the-cuff interviews on the parade route. My work will take all of one hour. They could throw in dinner with Tom Cruise and I'd still waver, because the Christmas parade is three thousand miles away.

It's drizzling on the morning of my departure. I nurse my baby in the blue light of dawn, play hide-and-seek behind the sofa cushions, feed him oatmeal, read and dance with him in the living room. I puree chicken for his next two lunches and dinners. Taxi's here. Dave holds Nicholas up to the screen door as I slip out onto the porch. I wave and blow them both kisses, then take a breath and dart down the wooden steps under a broken umbrella.

The moment the car door slams shut, I have a strange sense that this trip is no longer an option but a necessity.

My cab driver is a father of four whose attorney wife is home raising their kids while he works three jobs. The guy couldn't be happier. He informs me that if my baby ever threw up on an airplane, the flight attendants would rub dry coffee grinds all over my clothes to eliminate the smell.

"It's important to know these things," he assures me.

On board the overbooked flight, a three-month-old baby begins to cry as soon as the cabin doors close, and my milk comes down. I pump on an airplane for the first time. The little motor whirs, and white gold dribbles down into the plastic container under my navy blue airline blanket. The man seated across the aisle with his arms crossed against his chest pretends to be asleep. The seventy-something woman to my left is handwriting a eulogy for a lifetime friend. The twenty-something woman to my right is reading a book about God. The eight-year-old girl behind me, traveling alone, sings aloud with her headphones on. Across eight seats and two rows, over the sandy mountains of Nevada, I watch a father as he tries to soothe his baby.

I stare out the emergency-door window, imagining my son's face in the clouds. I've been gone exactly seven and a half hours. Is Nicholas becoming agitated? Is he getting cranky? Will Dave be able to console him? I stop myself. My stomach rumbles.

The flight attendant slowly walks down the aisle offering two packs of honey-roasted peanuts to each passenger, calling out in her high-altitude shorthand.

"Peanus?" she inquires, dropping the *t*. "Would you like peanus? Anybody want peanus? Peanus for you? Peanus?"

I reach for both packs from her manicured fingers, laughing to myself that as a tired, lactating mother worried about the effects of her thirty-nine-hour absence on her baby, the last thing on my mind is peanus.

The car that picks me up is driven by Steve, a tall, lanky guy with a thin, graying ponytail, a guy who has been to Woodstock but never had children.

"My sister's got three of 'em," he says chuckling. "I came darn close once. I got two cats."

My hotel room has that just-vacuumed aroma, a musty stench like the bag is full and the previous guest had French fries and lost a couple under the bed that the maid still hasn't found. I sit on the mattress, pull the toothpick out of my club sandwich, and keep glancing at the clock, doing the math. I am nearly oblivious to the fact that for the first time in nearly a year I am alone on a bed without a baby monitor.

The last numbers I remember seeing on the digital clock radio are 8:08. The next time I check, it is 4 a.m. I have just logged eight consecutive, uninterrupted hours of shut-eye. When I wake up, my body bounces off the mattress. No interim sitting to let the blood circulate before standing. No rubbing of the eyes to focus. I am simply lying down one second and standing the next in one fluid movement. I laugh out loud. The headache behind my eyes has at long last dissolved. I have *energy*.

I want to wear red.

For the first time in months, I can think clearly. Inhale without yawning. No stiff joints. No limping. Suddenly, I feel like Alice. It's as if I have walked through the mirror and visited my former life.

In my career life BC (Before Child), I had some interesting jobs. A talk show. A science show. A morning magazine show. Local and national, in cable and network. Television is a rather unpredictable business. Shows start up and get canceled. You can get bumped by game shows, soap operas, called to shoot pilots for promising new programs that either never get off the ground or take off only to land in a cornfield shortly thereafter.

I lived on the fly. Literally. I hosted a travel show for six years, and saw a fair bit of the globe. Quickly. Explored the Great Barrier Reef, one of the world's most stunning diving sites, in just under three hours. Visited Venice for about an hour. Stood at the Acropolis, the cradle of civilization, for a whole thirty minutes. I panned for gold for ten minutes in the Yukon. Rode a camel in Agadir. A helicopter in Alaska. A ski gondola in the French Alps. I spent so much time on airplanes that I once reached for my seat belt in a movie theater. It wasn't a glamorous gig by any means. You have to look fresh and be enthusiastic while your body argues vehemently with jet lag, migraines, the runs, hunger, poison ivy, dehydration, leg cramps. Or an allergy to the antimalaria pills that I had to take for seven weeks for a trip to West Africa, where I ingested an intestinal parasite in the Ivory Coast and subsequently spent three weeks in the hospital back home. (P.S. The show aired and looked lovely.)

The sun is shining the morning of the Christmas parade. I am squinting on Pier 39, wearing my red turtleneck and red gloves and red lips. Being around my baby, I have become accustomed to not wearing any makeup, hair spray, perfume, or heels, or clothes that need to be dry-cleaned. I have lived in flannel and cotton until this day when Mama's decked out like a Christmas tree on a Sunday morning by the bay. Every time I pass a parked car, I glance in the window and see two worlds collide.

After the parade, I have an hour before catching a ride to the airport, so I head back to my room, change, then hurry down to the pier for a bite. I have become used to eating en route or standing at the kitchen sink.

As I march along the boardwalk, I can hear my boot heels rhythmically clicking the pavement like a metronome on allegro. For the first time since Nicholas's birth, I linger.

I order some clam chowder in a sourdough bread bowl, a ham-and-Swiss sandwich, and a hot chocolate to go. I slurp and stroll, blowing at each spoonful, watching people pass me by. People pushing strollers. Mothers wearing their sleeping children. Small heads perched on big shoulders, tussled hair, little feet dangling from limp ankles. I know exactly how that feels now. How it fills the heart and breaks the back at the same time. How, no matter how tired you are, you somehow find the strength to totter another few steps, yards, city blocks, valleys with twenty-five pounds of baby in your arms.

I think about how I miss doing things, anything, in longer than fifteen-minute intervals. Like folding myself into an oversized couch and getting hopelessly lost inside the pages of a great book until the light disappears from the room.

Walking along Pier 39, I can see my baby's slate-blue eyes dancing, his arms waving at the sound of my hello, and my first and deepest instinct is to toss that gunnysack of flashbacks over my shoulder like a bridal bouquet and thank God a billion times over for leaving him with us. I smile at parents as they pass by with their babies as if I know them.

On my way back to the hotel, I feel somehow that all the parts of me have been reintroduced. My body and my spirit feel lighter. Since I became a mother eleven months ago, I realize that I have gradually begun to accept the fog in my head, the fog that eclipses my thoughts and clouds my emotions.

The fog may have impaired my vision back home, but on this radiantly bright morning along the wharf, I can see the Golden Gate Bridge. I can see giant, felt elf heads sitting in a heap by the orange parade pylons. I can see birds gliding across a sky so blue it looks like the painted backdrop in *Carousel*.

I feel as though I have just discovered a map, brushed away the dirt, and pulled my finger along the stretch of highway I am traveling. I heave the big dusty boulder out of my way.

Two blocks from the hotel, I pass a large family huddled under a traffic light on Jefferson Street, all six heads peering into a pop-up map of San Francisco. A few feet away, by the shrubs in front of a public parking lot, a young bearded man sits cross-legged on the sidewalk with his head down. His dry, cracked hands are folded in his lap, his bitten-down nails packed with dirt. A sign propped against his knee reads "Down vet. Please help." I drop a dollar in an empty paper cup held in place by a rock so the wind won't blow it away. He mutters, "God bless," as I walk by, and I imagine him as a baby, when he didn't know he'd someday be sitting on a slab of concrete in San Francisco with no home and a paper cup with a rock in it. I wonder where his mother is now.

I want to get home and hold my son.

I call Dave before I leave the hotel. Our baby is showing no apparent signs that he'll need therapy as a result of my thirty-nine-hour errand.

A few hours later, I stare long into the black sky from the window of my bulkhead seat, and wonder if I would or could ever do this again. My answer wavers between an unequivocal no, a definite maybe, and an irrepressible regret that this trip is nearing an end. I am determined to come home with my reintegrated parts and pick up where I left off on Pier 39.

The moment my plane touches down in New York at 10:30 p.m., it seems to me that I've been gone for ten minutes or two years. Everything looks new yet familiar, as if I have been beamed in and out of an alternate universe.

The next morning I anticipate a rousing welcome, a standing baby ovation that tells me my son is incredibly happy to see my face after thirty-nine hours at the grocery store. Instead, he looks at me and blinks a couple of times while he gnaws on his plastic yellow teether. We study each other's face. I search his for a sign of relief that I am home. I'll even settle for a scrap of recognition at this point.

He swaggers around the living room, grinning and drooling. John Wayne meets Charlie Chaplin. Two parts baby, one part baby penguin. As I stare at him, it dawns on me that the person I was actually worried about prior to takeoff thirty-nine hours ago was me.

My baby hadn't missed a beat.

I had expended such a ridiculous amount of emotional energy fretting over how my brief absence might affect my baby that I had grieved the loss *for* him. I had suffered my own absence. It occurred to me when I returned that I had, in fact, been worried about how *I* would do without *him*.

Nearly a year before this morning, I had assumed my role as mother and everything else fell away. I had systematically let the other parts of me collapse to make room for my baby.

I hadn't yet realized that there might be a distinction between my full experience of motherhood and my full expression as a person. I hadn't yet confronted the idea that there were as many roles as there were dreams in a person's life, that playing only a part of one's life script was like looking out a single window of a house forever and never seeing the backyard or the neighbor's tomato garden or how the world looked from the roof.

But finding my balance seems slippery. Like trying to grab a jellyfish in my fist. Sitting on the living-room carpet and watching Nicholas, I sense the presence of that elusive balance. Maybe I don't need to go three thousand miles away again to gain perspective. Pier 39 might well have been the local bookstore or the park or the overcrowded diner two blocks away.

But a few weeks later, g-force fatigue has crawled back into my veins. The daily grind. The rinse cycle. The lack of sleep. The baby's needs. Pier 39 seems to be a nice place I saw once in a travel magazine.

I feel my epiphany beginning to fade, like an incredibly vivid dream that you remember in uncanny detail the moment you wake up but that grows hazier the longer you're awake.

I can't figure out how or why the fog has rolled in again. Did it come when I wasn't looking—or when I was? Is it trying to obscure my vision or force me to look beyond what I can't see?

CHAPTER TWELVE

Water

need a haircut. My husband and son are at the park on a Saturday afternoon. I rush to the salon and fall back into the hairdresser's chair, breathless, weary, harried, feeling senselessly guilty for taking some time alone. At that moment, a slender blond woman I've never seen before appears in my mirror holding her little girl on one hip. I turn to smile at the baby as she passes by, and the woman stops to chat. I don't know yet that we are about to have a forty-five-minute conversation.

She and her one-year-old daughter have identical round gray-blue eyes framed by light eyebrows that curve down slightly toward the temples. It's her third child, ten years after her first.

She mentions her fatigue, tells me her age (thirty-seven), talks about how much she is enjoying her daughter, explains that she scheduled a C-section because her first two births were so complicated and risky, and is now thinking of having her scar removed.

"It's really thick and ribbony!" she says grimacing.

Her speech picks up speed. Her hair bounces around her jaw-bone as she speaks. She switches her baby to the other hip and gestures with her free hand.

"I swam for fifteen years before I had kids," she says, as if we have already been discussing swimming in some kind of context, which we haven't.

"I *love* swimming! It's just something I *need* to do, you know?"

Her eyes grow watery. She smiles as her voice gets louder, as if to camouflage her rage. Her baby and I glance at each other.

"I stopped swimming for a long time, because there was just no time to do it. But I told my husband I wanted to swim again, so I started to do it at night after the kids went to sleep. Well, you know what? I was dead at night. It didn't work. So I thought I'd do it early in the morning, like 6 a.m., before my husband went to work. Okay?"

I notice her eyes are red. She lowers her voice as she continues, like she is about to tell me a secret.

"My husband said to me, 'Geez, if I knew how much you loved swimming . . .,' and I said, 'What? You wouldn't have married me?' I mean, swimming is what I love to do! It's who I am! And he doesn't want me to do it, because it means *he* does more caretaking and *I* spend the one free hour I have in my day doing something for *me*!"

As she talks, my mind begins to drift. I can smell the chlorine, the damp air. I see her standing on the ledge, stashing her short blond waves under a cap, the snap of the rubber against her earlobes echoing between pool walls. I imagine her sending herself forward like an arrow. The water pulls her in, caresses her skin like a thousand warm hands. She is swimming, raging, weeping below the surface, where no one can hear her, where her tears are washed from her eyes, never seen. She swims for miles, to the deep end, across the English Channel, the Pacific, around the world, away, away. I hear the fury in the water around her, the rush of water past her ears, her cupped hands slicing the surface, finding her rhythm, lap after lap, until she stops to catch her breath at the wall.

Just as she does this afternoon talking to me.

"Anyhow," she says, shaking her head and limbs like she just got out of the pool, "you just have to do what you have to do, you know? I mean, if I don't take care of me, who *else* is going to?"

Her baby girl stares at me with such intensity, I think she might say something in an adult speaking voice. The three of us look at each other, then at the floor tiles, in silence.

CHAPTER THIRTEEN

Bath

have noticed that mothers who seem to have energy and bounce, whether working outside or inside the home, also have lovely feet. Magazine feet. Toenails the color of eggplant, bougainvilleas, the Mediterranean, fire trucks. Shiny as new coins.

I had my first pedicure when I was very, very pregnant, and I rather enjoyed the half hour of preening and reclining. I even picked a bold red geranium polish. It didn't matter. I couldn't *see* my feet once I stood up.

It's winter. I feel like an old broom. My boy is nearly a year old. My feet are in flannel socks that have lost their elasticity. I have finished packing our suitcases for our Christmas holiday down south, where we'll meet my parents, sister, and brother.

For my very special first Christmas as a tired new mother, my husband gives me a bath. A twenty-minute "destressing" bath at a spa. I haven't been to a spa in recent memory. In fact, I haven't had a bath in more than a year, though I *have* perfected the ninety-second shower.

"You will be transported," Dave says slowly, "to a place where you don't have to think of doing anything else but relaxing."

We pull up in front of a stately building, a sandblasted pink-granite facade, with two white columns on either side of an entrance that spans half a city block. Three massive queen palms stand outside the columns, their giant fronds bouncing breezily above the wrought-iron doors like they are waving me in. I glance over my shoulder to see if they might mean someone else.

"You're on vacation. Pick you up at five," my husband says smiling, as he and our baby drive off just before three o'clock on a Sunday afternoon. I walk up the *Gone with the Wind* staircase and stand for a moment at the top looking at all the loose change shimmering in the fountain below. I'm feeling oddly out of place when I am greeted by Daniel.

"You've *never* had a spa bath?" he asks incredulously.

"Never."

"Never?" he insists, like I'm pulling his leg.

"Never."

"What about a gommage?" he asks.

"A who?"

"Gommage. It's a European cleansing and sloughing treatment for the skin. A rich exfoliating cream is applied to the body and then showered off. You're then cocooned in a plankton body mask."

"Plankton?"

"Mm-hmm. The mask is painted on quickly with a two-inch pony-hair brush. You're then wrapped with slightly damp, heavy white linens—two to three sheets. And, on top of that, a thermal blanket for about ten minutes. It's like being tucked in by your mother! As if you're going back into some embryonic state. I'm sure it must trigger some type of back-to-the-womb feeling."

Plankton?

Once inside the spa, I am escorted to a waiting area that smells like laundry still warm from the dryer. I recline on a white chaise longue by the half-moon bay window, flanked by white orchids in small pots. On the coffee table are a tall glass pitcher of water with floating cucumber slices, a tray of purple grapes, ripe pears, yellow and green apples. My mind wanders. *I'm not used to this. I could get used this.* I sip cucumber water. I write. I nibble. I glance at my watch.

"Hi, I'm Stacy," says a young woman who sounds just like Susan Sarandon. I follow her to a small, dimly lit chamber, where she fills a deep tub with hot water and lights candles around the room.

"Do you like it hot or very hot?" she asks.

"Not too hot."

"Would you like a soothing or a restorative bath?" she inquires.

"Soothing *or* restorative?"

"Yes, you can choose which bath you'd like."

I pause.

"Can I have both?" I ask, wanting *all* the candy.

"Not really," she says, like one could not be both soothed and restored at the same time. As if mixing the potions was highly flammable.

"The soothing bath uses essence of lavender and counteracts the effects of stress," she says, "and the restorative bath uses essences of orange and ylang-ylang to relieve tension and replace minerals lost from pollution and exposure to the elements."

I can't fathom the explanation. Soothing or restorative, I wonder. To be soothed or restored. Does it have to be this complicated?

I choose the soothing bath because Nicholas's eyelids were lavender when he was born, because I spend all day soothing him, because my tired body wants a balm, because my spirit feels like cargo.

I watch Stacy's long fingers empty two tiny brown vials into my bath like a laboratory chemist. She twists the timer to the right, flips a switch, and whispers out the door with the fluid movement of a ballerina.

We are finally alone, me and the raging bath, the fury of eight water jets making so much noise that it almost seems silent. I begin to submerge. I have twenty minutes ahead of me.

Twenty minutes.

A whole eighteen and a half minutes longer than I have had in the shower all year. Here I am, being pummeled by water, imagining my husband and baby out there strolling in search of Ben and Jerry's ice cream. Imagining all the women in adjacent chambers being hydrated, cleansed, exfoliated, peeled, polished, wrapped, toned, refreshed, rejuvenated, soothed, and restored. Thinking of how quickly this holiday will pass. Feeling assaulted already by the piles of unwashed laundry waiting in the wicker hamper back home.

I close my eyes. I have a hard time imagining the idea of being "restored." What does that look like? Feel like? Restore what? I wonder.

I knew a woman whose boyfriend was the restoration director for the Metropolitan Museum in New York. I knew a man who restored buildings, trying to preserve their original state. And I knew a photographer who restored old photos.

"Restore" means to put back into place, to bring into use or being again, to bring back to a healthy state, to recreate the original form. I begin to wonder about *my* original form. Will I be restored, put back into place? Restored to what exactly?

How does a person, a mother, know when she needs restoration? What are her clues? Symptoms? Hunches? Is it obvious, like a rash? Or unseen, like private grief? Did it occur as a pattern or a big event? A series of experiences or one major meltdown? Would she restore herself or have someone do it for her? To her? Is it a one-time event or a work-in-progress, like a site under construction? When does she know she has been restored?

And what if she could never return to her original form completely? What if that form, that state of being, that "place" no longer existed since she walked through the one-way door into motherhood?

I am Gumby walking down the hall, all rubber, no knees. Angie, the spa pedicurist, is a friendly woman with kind blue eyes. Her hair is slicked back in a blond ponytail, her toes adorned with silver rings.

She has the kind of face that says, C'mon, talk to me, and start with the bad stuff so we can get it out of the way.

After my twenty-minute bath, I sit down and present her my right foot, like Cinderella at midnight. She tells me about her fiancé who can't commit, his family who hates her, the fights they've had about loyalties and frailties, his fear of his mother's disapproval, her concern about his mother's rejection of her, their elusive wedding date, her fiancé's inability to confront his family's attempts at exclusion, her love for their two Labradors, eleven and nine in dog years, and her distant longing for a baby.

"I don't know how I'd do it," she says. "We go away for two days, and I miss the dogs so terribly; it's nearly unbearable."

I stare hypnotically as she paints my toenails in slow motion, carefully, precisely, as if she were painting Ukrainian Easter eggs.

It's my turn to share intimate details with this person I've known for twelve minutes. I tell her that I love my son so much it hurts sometimes. That, yes, I'm home with him, but I know mothers who work ten hours a day in an office who also suffer from terrible pangs of loss and guilt. I tell her how when I am apart from my baby, like now, I think I hear the clear bell of his needs clanging ever so faintly, like in a church steeple miles away.

I tell her about how edgy and irritable I have been feeling lately. How tired I am of my baby's insistent, escalating wail that makes my throat tight and my ears hot with fear and shame. I tell her how, despite respecting his needs, I can feel both bound by them yet compelled from the deepest place in me to answer them.

I tell her how the voices can get under my skin sometimes. The voices that warn me of power struggles ahead, of spoiled children like food left out in the sun. The voices that seem to chant more loudly whenever I feel weary and ambivalent.

I tell her that when I occasionally work on brief projects away from home for the day, I feel alive and vital, my spirit feels free to fly, but after a while, I worry that I've gone too far, and I begin to feel untethered, yearning for home and the weight of my baby in my arms.

I tell her how I feel strange every time I leave him for more than a few hours, as though I am *missing a limb*. And suddenly I notice, as she files and scrapes and nods empathetically, that she has no ring finger. I mean, the whole finger is . . . gone. My foot is in her palm as I whine about missing limbs, and here is this gracious woman with a fiancé, no wedding date, no engagement ring—and no ring finger.

The night before my bath, Dave and I take a barefoot walk along the beach under the largest, brightest moon in a hundred and thirty-three years, while Nicholas sleeps at the hotel with my parents. It is our first vacation since our son was born, and my mind feels like my printer when the paper jams. It's also our first night alone, just the two of us, in nearly a year, and I can't shake the feeling that I have to be somewhere else.

Here we are rambling along the shore, Dave sipping warm port from a plastic cup and me kicking seashells.

"Where are you right now?" he asks.

"What do you mean?"

"Your feet are walking on the sand, but where are *you?*"

"I just wonder if the baby . . .," I mumble.

Dave sighs. Not the "Gosh I'm pooped" kind of sigh. Or the "Have you seen my wallet?" sigh. But that sigh that says "Are you ever going to stop obsessing over the baby and pay a crumb of attention to me for the rest of our married lives?" *That* kind of sigh.

I sigh in return. Before long, the two of us are conversing in sighs, breathing in and puffing air every few minutes while the waves lap at our feet. I suddenly remember our good pals who once had an underwater argument after they had lost sight of the boat on a scuba-diving excursion. I always thought that was bizarre until this night.

The moon lights up the beach like a giant follow spot, but I still can't see where I am going. I try to sort through the tangle of my maternal emotions. Part of it is that I can't believe that we actually have babies and don't have them attached to us as a body part for all of eternity. I feel slightly off-kilter without my baby, as if I have left something hanging in midair. Myself, maybe.

And yet, I feel desperate for a little time alone. It's difficult for me to leave the baby these days because he's teething madly, and he'll cry that relentless cry for Mommy who won't be there. Even though I know that from here on in, our hearts are bound to break again and again. It is so impossible to avoid, and still something about the sheer impracticality of being able to be there whenever he needs me makes me feel terribly sad and displaced at this moment in time.

I'm tired. Lack of sleep is only a fraction of it. I'm tired of comparing my son to the ones that sleep the night, smile at strangers, and enjoy transportation, restaurants, diaper changes, baths, pediatricians. And I'm tired of pretending I don't. I'm tired of trying so hard to defend my son's needs in the face of a doubting crowd, tired of wondering if they might be right. And tired of not always believing in my own intuition and my own child. I'm tired of riding the brakes.

I have come to know all of my baby's subtle cues and nameless anxieties, and after nearly a year of practice, I can crack his secret code like a cat burglar blindfolded with one hand tied behind my back. I know what *he* needs, but I have started to lose touch with what *I* need. And worse, I have begun to occasionally feel the quiet ache of indifference. Sometimes, I feel that the only way I can answer his needs is to ignore my own, as though our needs were mutually exclusive.

I shake my head in disbelief. Is this who I have become? How on earth did I get *here?*

Our sighs have ceased. We talk long into the bright night about expecting and expectations, fantasy and reality, the politics of give-and-take. The ocean listens. Our mouths grow dry and salty. The winds pick up, and for a moment it seems as if they are carrying our words out to sea, sentence by sentence, blowing away our veils until our beating hearts are finally free to tell the story.

Stacy kneads my back, working it like a giant slab of bread dough, and explains in a gentle voice that she chose peppermint oil to give me energy and lavender oil to relax me. I can barely speak, but I want to ask her if maybe the two oils could cancel each other out. The smell of peppermint nauseates me. Maybe it's the rubdown right after the hot bath. I hear my voice talking far away, like I am speaking in another room, and I can hear myself through the wall. She offers to add a little essence of orange and ylang-ylang.

But I don't need an essence or a potion. Restoration, I realize, is an inside job.

At our church back home, Reverend Jim speaks of the "breath of life" in his sermon. He talks about getting refreshed, restored, and "resouled." My ears perk up as if I've just heard a familiar language in a foreign country.

He talks about catching our breath and finding our peace. About "regaining our identity as human beings reanimated by the breath of life." And he urges us—me—to cultivate a discipline, an openness to discover that identity.

And I'm listening to these words as I hold my breath.

I realize that somehow my breathing seems to have gotten more shallow with each month. The more my baby grows, the less I seem to breathe.

"Remember to *breathe*," Reverend Jim says.

And I suck in the deepest breath of the year so far. I begin to feel my extremities again, my limbs connected to my body, the rush of blood through my veins. The breath of life. My life. Nicholas's life.

I feel an energy surging through me like an electric current. There's something about the power of a hot bath and red toenails that makes me want to tap my full creativity, dream big, and take each day as another chance to see—and *be*—anew.

CHAPTER FOURTEEN

Labor After Delivery

have a job interview. I feel strangely like Gilligan. Do I want to be rescued from the Isle of Motherhood? Of course not. Do I want a sometime outlet where I can express myself in ways that require clean clothes and full, grammatically correct sentences? Bring it on.

It's a hosting position on a new show about motherhood. I would tape only a few days every month, an ideal schedule for my baby and me. The meeting is booked for 11 a.m. in two weeks. I'll have Maggie, our occasional babysitter, come to watch Nicholas. She's the only person with whom he seems to feel comfortable other than family.

On the morning of my interview, I lay out my taupe suit and brush the dust off the shoulders when the phone rings. It's Maggie. Her daughter's sick and she's really, really sorry but . . .

I call the nice Madison Avenue people to tell them that I have a baby, that I have no backup, that I am really, really sorry but . . .

And then, I hear two words that make no sense to me whatsoever.

"Bring him?" I ask, as if I were just asked to pole-vault naked over an electrical fence.

Preparing to go to this interview is not unlike packing for a very long trip to another country. Besides the baby's diapers and wipes, I have his car seat, his favorite books (*Jamberry; Mr. Brown Can Moo, Can You?; Great Day for Up*), his elephant and frog teethers, familiar toys and Winnie-the-Pooh rattle socks, a baggie of Cheerios, three jars of baby food, Tupperware, a bib, a spoon, two bottles, a *Baby Mozart* video, and a portable playpen.

Nicholas naps on the cab ride into Manhattan. The cabbie tells me he is forbidden by law to leave his taxi to help me, so I haul each piece of baby gear from the curb to the lobby, with the baby perched on my left hip.

People in the pink marble foyer of the Madison Avenue office building rush to the elevators with their Palm Pilots and wafer-thin cell phones, their heels echoing as they click on the floor tiles. They smell like chardonnay and cigars, pricey cologne, grilled seafood.

Nobody smells like Balmex.

I suddenly feel like a bag lady with her baby and their ten worldly possessions. People seem to be avoiding me, ignoring me, walking around, past, through me. Nicholas begins to whimper.

Then, in some bizarre twist of fate, I spot the man who is about to interview me. He is talking with another gentleman by the guard's desk in the lobby. Oh, here he comes. Uh-oh, he sees me. The elevator doors are parting. And here we are—me, my baby, my potential boss, and enough stuff to start a yard sale—all riding north together in a mirrored box with fake wood moldings on the corner of Madison and Sixty-first.

On the twenty-third floor, in the conference room, my thirteen-month-old wants to walk, touch the plants, grab the papers on the table. I set up the playpen and set him up with an ample supply of toys, pop-up books, Cheerios, water, teethers, a toothbrush, floss, the *New York Times Book Review,* a personal journal, a yoga mat, and some prayer beads, but he stands in the corner closest to my chair, his little hands clasping the plastic blue railing, looking like a puppy at the pound.

"Up?" he asks softly, his blue eyes looking around the unfamiliar room of executive faces and mahogany furniture.

"Nicholas, buddy?" each person bellows in turn, trying to distract him. They don't know that he doesn't fall for that stuff. Just like he doesn't pose for pictures, high-five, blow a kiss on request, or play "peek" with people he doesn't know. Yes, this baby needs to know you before he plays peekaboo with you.

The executive people need to talk with me, review scripts, and ask me questions. Nicholas needs to talk with me too, review his books, and ask me questions. So, sitting high above Madison Avenue on the edge of my swivel chair surrounded by crushed Cheerios, I attempt to do both.

In a hushed voice, I read a rhyme from *Jamberry*.

One berry two berry pick me a blueberry . . .

Then I look at the executive people and discuss show content and format in my normal speaking voice.

Raspberry jazzberry razzamatazzberry . . .

Then I listen attentively to their job description, their expectations of me, and the potential shooting schedule.

Blackberry trackberry, clickety-clackberry . . .

I'm surprised that it actually works quite well for about five and a half minutes.

"He's a bundle!" a woman says, with a grin and a raised brow. I can feel myself crouching in the foxhole.

"Yeah," I reply. "He's got a lot of energy."

Nicholas is growing increasingly unhappy with the whole charade. He wants out.

But the interview and script-reading haven't even begun. People kindly offer to hold him, carry him, rock him. But Nicholas isn't the kind of guy you pass around at a party. My potential boss puts him on his lap for a second, and my son looks at him square in the eye, as if to say, I've never seen you before in my life. And you're *not* my father.

I can feel my upper lip break out into a sweat. I smile demurely like I do this all the time, like I am not the least bit uncomfortable about the fact that my baby is now being interviewed for the job.

Dave is on a construction site a mile away. He is wearing a hardhat and earmuffs, supervising the building according to his architectural plans. He has a pager.

It's my last resort.

It's lunchtime. The building site will be quiet for about an hour. My husband happily struts uptown to the pink marble foyer and rides the elevator to the conference room, where Nicholas greets him with a thousand-watt smile. The executive people give Dave a warm, appreciative welcome, shaking his hand in that "Nice to meet you, Mel Gibson" kind of way. No, Nelson Mandela. No, no, Paul the Apostle.

They have formed a semicircle around him while he holds Nicholas in his arms and chats nonchalantly about architecture, the weather, the Dow Jones, and the magic of fatherhood. Then he and our son slip out of the conference room to an empty office down the hall, where our baby falls asleep in his arms while Dave finishes a sandwich and I finish my interview. As he leaves, the executive people thank him profusely for saving the day, while I collapse the playpen, gather baby paraphernalia, brush away Cheerio dust, and wipe the sweat from my upper lip.

It's not that I don't absolutely appreciate my husband's support and help. Lord knows I do. He *did* save the day, or the meeting anyway. It's just that it might have seemed to the Madison Avenue executives that I could not.

"Bring him," they said.

They had no idea that Nicholas is not the kind of baby who can sit in his car seat on the conference-room floor and stare at his thumbs for the better part of an hour. I feel momentarily embarrassed that he isn't who they need him to be, resentful that they want him to be someone else, defensive of his right to be himself, and fiercely proud of who he is.

After the meeting, I kiss Dave good-bye; get myself, Nicholas, and our yard sale into a cab; and head across town to the lot on Fifty-eighth Street where Dave has parked our car.

The moment I buckle Nicholas into his car seat, I sense an invisible hourglass turn upside down. We start up the West Side Highway pretty smoothly, but by mile six, he has gone full tilt. There are no shoulders on this road, no rest stops, no safe places to pull over whatsoever. With my eyes shifting from the road to the rearview to the traffic ahead back to the car clock and the rearview again, I sing, talk, reassure him, extend my right arm to the back seat, and caress his shins and knuckles as a river of mucus bubbles out of his nose, as he cries hysterically the whole ten miles back to our driveway.

As soon we are outside, free of car-seat straps and crowds and unfamiliar people trying to be familiar, he falls asleep. I carry him up the wooden stairs to our front door. After I lay him in his crib, I fall facedown into the couch. My feet throb from the leather boots I wore on the sidewalks of Manhattan. My ears ring from the cab horns. Home is my cocoon where I savor the silence, the carpet under my bare toes. Who am I kidding? I'll go back to work later, when Nicholas is older, when I'm older, when I have even less energy than I do now.

The telephone rings the next morning. I got the job, a pilot for a show that, in the end, never finds an airwave. I feel a sense of relief, like when a snowstorm closes school down for the day.

Later that evening, I find out that I am scheduled to be executed at 9 p.m. by an old colleague of mine—a television critic—in front of a large crowd in a public atrium. I don't know why my life is over. I ask around. One person, a woman, smirks and says nothing. I feel powerless. My only hope is to ask an attorney if he could convince the judge to overturn the decision.

"You have a point," he responds. "Besides I want to keep you working for years to come."

I wake up with a start.

It's 5:50 a.m. I can't sleep anymore. Twenty minutes later, my toddler is up for the day.

My cold palms are wrapped around a hot mug of tea at a friend's crowded apartment on a bright and crisp morning in New York. Dave, Nicholas, and I have been invited for Sunday brunch. The living-room air is filled with the voices of strangers and the aroma of banana muffins. There are day traders here, a retail buyer, a publicist, two financial advisers, a history professor, a corporate lawyer, a realtor.

A thirty-something gentleman in a black turtleneck and gray tweed jacket asks me what I do. Well, I'm a mother, I say for starters. But somewhere between the word "mother" and the words that follow, the conversation has ended. He thinks I'm a good person without ambition, knowledge, or power.

He thinks of me in a box. Four walls. A stay-at-*home* mother.

He assumes that if he stands there much longer, I'll start playing peekaboo with him. I want to open my mouth and unravel my tongue into the air like a giant red carpet, and spew, "I *know* things!" I want to tell him the Nasdaq is up, and his fly is down. I want to humiliate him for dismissing me. Or is it me dismissing myself?

Having an identity never seemed to be an issue for me in the workplace. I only began to seriously question it when the work I was doing was for an audience of one, a small helpless creature whose idea of feedback was spit-up.

Before I had a baby, I wanted to make a name for myself. I found an identity in a title, in the eyes of others, on a payroll, engraved on an award. And yet, as hard as I worked to be Somebody, I really had no clue who I was until I became a mother and felt like my identity went missing. Is it because I lost it—or is it that I never had it in the first place?

———

I have friends who put their careers aside or on hold in order to raise children. Fashion designer, video producer, news anchor, illustrator, obstetrician, defense attorney, magazine editor, teacher, runway model. My friend Maria produced stories for television newsmagazines before she had Alexander. Jennifer passed up a job as a fashion director for a magazine to stay home with Max. Nina traveled the world designing fabrics before her twins came along. Some of my friends stayed home for a year, some for three years, and some until their babies went to college.

I also know many devoted mothers who went back to work because they had jobs that they had worked long and hard to procure, for which they had spent years in graduate school; jobs that offered them tenure, pension, lifelong security, benefits; jobs that meant food on the table, heat in the house, and a working telephone. And I know others who went back to work right away because they could not stand the thought of being with the baby all day.

"I know *I* couldn't do it," my husband admits, swigging his coffee. He is referring to being home with the baby. And I remember when I didn't think I could either. Just yesterday afternoon, for example.

When you find yourself at the brink on a daily basis, pushed way past your point of no return—that individual, purely subjective point where your spirit feels broken in an utterly heart-wrenching way you could have never imagined when you were pregnant—when you must nonetheless come up with the goods to be a responsible, compassionate, loving parent, you are then required to reach beyond your despair and pull yourself back from the edge where the smallest successful moment of mothering feels like a worldly triumph and the brief moments of intolerance feel like the worst failures of humanity.

"I could *never* stay home," says Julie, a visiting thirty-five-year-old events planner who works in Los Angeles. "I'd go crazy!"

She has meetings booked from breakfast to dusk.

"Mommy, *I* want to be your meeting," her three-year-old son recently said into the telephone receiver after dinner.

Julie thinks I've squandered my talents, wasted the best years of my life changing diapers, nursing on demand, answering my son's needs at the expense of my own. She hates to wonder about how much better off my son might be down the road because of my choice to stay home. I am loath to think of how much better off she might be right now because of her decision to carve a piece of the pie for herself.

We terrify each other.

I vacillate between never wanting to work again and feeling oppressed by the thought of never working again. It isn't about a job. It's about the place I go to in my head when I'm not folding kitchen towels into rectangles and making sweet-potato puree and rocking the baby at 3:23 a.m. I need to peer beyond these walls. Is that necessarily outside the house? Society wants me to be doing something in the labor force on a payroll in order that I may be perceived as a professional. Am I a mother who *used to be* a journalist? Used to think? To create? Or am I now a woman who procreates?

The baby becomes the focus, the blank canvas (or so we presume) upon which we sketch our stories. Before motherhood, we talked about our jobs, our bosses, our assignments and accomplishments. Now our achievements are tightly swaddled in our baby's development.

About a month after the brunch, I receive a phone call from a television producer I have never met who has booked me to do a series of interviews for a special on the world's great architects.

"But you haven't checked with me first to see if I'm available," I say, stupefied that he would have skipped that obvious step in the process.

"Listen," he cuts in, "I'm trying to get you *out* of the house."

He assumed I would jump at any chance to put on real shoes and go to the Big City to talk with Interesting People, since, after all, I *am* at home all day studying carpet fibers with the baby.

It isn't that different when he is a she. A few weeks later, another producer calls me wondering what those in the industry will think when they hear I have not been "working" for the past couple of years.

"Perception is reality," she says. "And they might perceive that your absence decreases your market value."

My inner pit bull begins to foam at the mouth.

"Do I have less ability than I did before I conceived a child?" I retort. "Did having a baby strip me of my knowledge? Do employers respect a woman more if she treats her baby as if he were a casual addition to her life? Would I appear stronger, more professional, if I went back to work three days after giving birth? *Are you telling me to forget about it, to consider myself unemployable from here on out?*"

I fire these questions at her in one breath.

"I'm just saying that I can't guarantee that I can find something for you, especially if you want a job where you can still spend time with your baby," she says with the feigned, forced diplomacy of a telemarketer who is being recorded. "I think it's wonderful that you chose to stay home. I just think the industry might wonder where you fit into things now."

I listen to her distant voice explaining the law of diminishing returns as it applies to work and motherhood. The longer I am out of the labor force, she calculates, the less likely I will be able to return to it. Producer and I exchange good-byes. I sit slumped on the edge of my bed in a nauseous funk.

Then I suddenly remember my dream. The atrium. The critic. The scheduled execution. The attorney. The judge.

I sit upright. No alarm clock could have sounded this wake-up call.

I didn't so much dream I was going to be executed as I dreamed other people had the power to give me life or take it away—to judge me and my life as worthy (or not) of making a contribution. That wasn't the pineapple on my pizza, either. *I* wrote that script. My unconscious pen. In the hidden dungeon of my mind, these self-perceptions lie shackled and well fed.

It occurs to me that realizing one's potential is not something concrete that we can put off until we have more time, but something deeply internal that we must explore every day of our lives, regardless of poopy diapers and dirty laundry. This is work I must do in my head and my heart, not something that requires a passport and a month off.

I must rake through fears of commitment and intimacy, success and failure, courage and cowardice, conviction and ambivalence.

I hear the charge. The dream is a call to action.

If the sky's the limit, I have to quit staring at the ceiling. If not, how can I give my own child the wings to fly beyond it?

The phone rings. A possibility to host a television special. Two weeks away in China.

"Do it!" squeals my friend Amanda. "Go! *Go!*"

"Babies have no concept of time," says my friend Diane. "He won't even realize you're gone."

"I'm breast-feeding," I remind her.

"Oh, he'll go on a nursing strike for sure when you get back," she predicts.

And we joke about Nicholas picketing in his diaper outside our apartment. NO MORE BOOBY! DOWN WITH BOOBY!

"That's far," worries Laurie. "What if you had to get back quickly? What if there was trouble there? What if it was—"

"A chance of a lifetime," says Diane.

"You *have* to go," orders Amanda.

But I can't. She looks at me as if I have just won the lottery and ripped up the ticket. But to me, this debate isn't about the paycheck or the playpen. It's about whether or not we can live well with our choices.

Are we doing the right thing for our baby? For ourselves? What *is* right? Do we calculate our legitimacy by what other mothers have chosen, by how our child is faring, by how *we* feel—or a combination of all three?

Can I choose and then accept my choice without holding myself hostage by the chains of self-doubt? It's clear to me now. The universe responds to us when we have already chosen—when we have decided, in a moment of grace, to open ourselves up fully to our own possibilities. When we stop waiting for others to define our lives, to correct our mistakes, to change our circumstances. When we start living our own truth, following our own intuition, mustering courage to live without guilt and find a little joy in the process of our unfolding.

The focus shifts from whether I will work again (or whether someone out there thinks I'm worth hiring), to *how* I want to work, why I want to work, and what I want to do. Maybe I want to invent something, write a children's book, open a restaurant, design an educational toy, work with parents and children. This isn't about "having it all." It's about making a life, not a living, as my old friend Robert used to say.

Now, *therein* lies an identity. Not in the task, the title, or the assignment, but in the full investigation of our mixed emotions at every crossroads until, detour by detour, we discover the path to our true self.

My ambivalence has nothing to do with how much I love my

child. It's not that I wish for another life or even regret the road taken, but rather that I am coming to understand the staggering complexity of our needs. This is much deeper than a mere choice between home or the workplace.

Before motherhood, I measured my growth by my earnings, my outcome by my income. But on the most successful day in my career, I still never felt like I had truly made a difference. The most prestigious position I have held never once made me feel as though I was part of a larger whole. I never felt eternity as a professional. I never suffered the shameful despair of wanting to quit and the itchy panic of knowing I could not take a tidy little leave of absence or change jobs altogether. I never felt the permanence of being loved. I never cared so much how somebody else was feeling. I never prayed for someone else first.

Sometimes, though, I am wistful, yearning for a time when I felt important in the eyes of others. Then I remind myself that I have never been more important than in the eyes of this small boy. And I was never as important at the office as I might have liked to believe.

Looking at my life before and after baby—at labor before and after delivery—I realize now that being a mother has given me an opportunity that I never had in the sixteen years I worked before I had a baby: a chance to connect. To commit. To confront myself. To learn how to give without regret and receive without apology. To separate identity from image, and be accountable for who I am, not just what I do.

Year Two

CHAPTER FIFTEEN

Fear Not (Eventually)

e venture south, all the way to the end of our street where the bulrushes meet Interstate 95. When the bulrushes part, Nicholas and I can see the eighteen-wheelers and oil tankers zooming by. I lock the wheel brakes and squat beside my son. He leans forward into the scenery, a spectator at Wimbledon, lips pursed like he's sucking a lozenge. I watch him for an hour without noticing my legs are asleep.

Strolleritis is cured.

Somewhere back in Nicholas's eighth month of life, the stroller tires went from being shiny black treads clean enough to lick, to well-worn wheels with mud, grass, and chewed gum in the grooves. Now, five months shy of two, he cries when I take him *out* of the stroller.

What was strolleritis all about? We will never know, though he will be fully interrogated at the kitchen table before getting his driver's license. The mysterious allergy to the bath subsides after about three months, and the car allergy after about seven. We actually go to the grocery store together—park the car, walk the aisles, gather and pay for food, and drive home—for the first time at eight months. Blenders, washing machines, lawn mowers, hair dryers, and various other appliances, however, take a little longer.

———

I present to the court Exhibit A, the Hoover. Forty-one inches tall, dark green, with a black handle and four handsome nozzle attachments.

My son is eight weeks old the first time he hears the switch flipped on. You'd think someone had started up a buzzsaw in the living room. Nicholas shakes like it's the devil incarnate. Just glancing at Hoover standing upright in the back of the dark closet makes him hyperventilate. Apparently, babies love the vacuum's "white noise." To my baby, it's the official boogeyman.

Over the months, I watch my son move through several distinct stages.

Stage 1, Cling and Clean: I become adept at running the vacuum down the hall, across the living-room floor, and into two bedrooms while holding Nicholas in one arm and singing lilting nursery rhymes over the roar of the machine. He clings to me while I clean the house in under a minute.

Stage 2, Cling-free and Curious: He sidesteps toward the closet door suspiciously, tentatively, to check on the vacuum's whereabouts. I can now run Hoover without holding Nicholas, but he runs from the machine, hiding behind doors and furniture to avoid its wrath.

Stage 3, Confrontation: He becomes fixated on Hoover. On some mornings, his first word of the day is "bakoom," as if it was on his mind all night. He tiptoes to the closet, peering past the doorknob into the darkness. "Ba-kooom?" he says under his breath, waiting for an answer. He tries to make contact with it, determine its intentions here in our house. Over the next few weeks, he slowly opens the door and finally stands face-to-face with Hoover.

"Das a ba-koom," he says, pointing to the appliance, telling it what it is in case it didn't know—letting it know that *he* knows. The vacuum says nothing. My son is getting loose with it, tapping its neck, then retracting his hand quickly before it can bite him.

Stage 4, Casual Acquaintances: While I vacuum, he now runs in front of Hoover, alongside it, away from it, as if the two of them are playing appliance tag. He does not cry anymore when I turn on the machine. He has begun to befriend Hoover, though he's not completely sure he trusts it.

Stage 5, Civic Duty: When my sister Nora, his Auntie Noo Noo, comes to visit, Nicholas greets her immediately—"Ba-koom"—then looks around mysteriously and cues her to follow him down the hall to the master bedroom, into the corner where the closet door is suspiciously closed. He warns, "Dat's a ba-koom," like he's saying, "Look, I need to let you know there's a vacuum in this house." Noo plays right along, inching surreptitiously toward the culprit, letting Nicholas be her trusty guide.

Stage 6, Domestic Help: At this point, he begs me to push Hoover himself. He wants me to back off and get my grubby fingers off *his* machine. He wails when I turn the switch off. "More vacu-umeeming, Mah-mee!"

Stage 7, Hoover Live Unplugged: Now, he stands in front of the closet door's full-length mirror impersonating Elvis using the microphone he has fashioned out of the vacuum hose and two brush attachments.

My earliest fear was Bozo the Clown. I was four. Thirty years later, it's heights. After living eight miles from midtown Manhattan for ten years, I've yet to visit the top of the Empire State Building.

My son's earliest fear was the bath. And the stroller. The car. Diaper changes. Noise. Strangers. Crowds. Restaurants. Household appliances. It would be many months before he would relinquish any of them.

When my baby came into the world with provisos, terms and conditions, fine print, notwithstanding clauses, and batteries not included, he needed his environment as simple as possible. At first I thought I could change him—or should. As if his fears were flaws.

"A baby who hates the bath? *And* the stroller? *And* the car?" people would say to me incredulously. "That's *bizarre!*"

What they were really saying was, "*He's* bizarre!" At least that's how I heard it.

Defensive of my son's right to a bona fide quirk and secretly worried about his future as a recluse, I wondered if his mysterious sensitivities to sound, strangers, transportation, and change would amount to a lifetime of neuroses.

His fears stir mine. I wonder what his aversions say about him—and about me. A fearful child might hold himself back, I fret. A fearful child might hold *me* back, I confess to myself.

It occurs to me that my perception of his fears might mess with his experience of them. A bulky tangle of his and my anxieties, expanding like a giant Chia pet.

Can't I just allow him to be afraid of the slide, the dog, the water without judging it as wrong? Unjustified? Weak? And who would *I* be to determine that? Me, the one who'd rather swim naked in an icy fjord than get into a cramped elevator.

I decide to stop seeing his fears as obstacles and start perceiving them as markers along the road, positive signs that he is processing his world. Fears for the moment. Legitimate. Real. Ephemeral. Maybe more importantly, I decide to listen to my own fears, how they may be woven into the fabric of my parenting.

A woman I met at a playground watched her five-year-old boy climb a short branch of a tree.

"Don't you worry that he might fall and hit his head on one of those boulders?" I asked politely.

Sandy smiled graciously and said, "I think if a child hears our warning to be careful every five minutes, and sees how anxious we are that he might fall, then he may very well fall because we expect him to. And he may just stop trying things altogether."

Her son didn't look any more athletic or coordinated than the average child of that age, but there was something in his face. A generosity of spirit, a quiet confidence. I watched his dismount. Sandy had two fingers over her mouth in a hushing pose, as if to remind her lips not to speak. He slid down from the branch slowly, carefully, methodically.

At nineteen months, Nicholas is too young to climb a tree, but like most children, and certainly many boys, he is irrepressibly drawn to dirt, sticks, and the obvious combination of the two, digging. On one of our midday stick hunts, he is elated to find a broken branch that measures his height. I want to say, be careful. But I refrain and instead follow his train of thought. Silently, he proceeds to drill the stick into the soil by a nearby tree. I want to remind him to watch out for the flowers. But before I can say anything about respecting property and minding the garden and watching his toes and not falling forward to poke his eye out, he finds a free patch of dirt away from the daffodils, places himself a few inches from the stick now standing vertically in the dirt, picks up a small five-inch twig from the ground, takes one step backward, and stops. Before I can break the humid afternoon silence, he begins to sing into the long stick "microphone" while strumming the small stick "guitah." Once he is done, he pulls the stick out of the ground and places it under a tree so it doesn't "ouch" him.

And I remember the day, several months ago, when I woke up with laryngitis. With no voice at all, I wondered how on earth I was going to parent a toddler. Then, I listened with amazement as Nicholas whispered to me, adapted his level of activity, his volume, and his energy to meet mine.

"Dooty," he said at the park, pointing to the straw and cup littered on the ground.

"Cah-fu," he warned himself as he stepped over some stones.

"Dan-juss," he says, gesturing to a steep embankment leading to the babbling brook behind a wire fence.

If I had been able to talk that day, I would have simply told him what he already *knew*. I wondered how I might replace those words, and find new ways of relating to him. I learned something about parenting ruts and the importance of self-mastery in the life of a toddler.

Witnessing my son's conquest of Hooverphobia opened my eyes to overcoming my own fears. I once thought of fear as an immobilizer. I can see now that in light of our discomfort with our own adult fears, we tend to be put off by other people who seem apprehensive or fearful—including our own children.

I can see how their fears remind us of ours, and how our own unwieldy, unresolved anxieties could get nudged awake by these little twenty-five-pound citizens who look to us for security. We worry about their safety. We worry about their personalities, wondering whether our son will be a loner or our daughter will grow into a woman who lets others cast her aside. We worry that their childhood fears might be permanent. That those fears may brand them for life. Put a lid on their (our) dreams. Exclude them from the team, the prom, the promotion. No successful executive or entrepreneur is a scaredy-cat.

It's a scorchingly hot summer day, the kind that fogs your sunglasses the moment you walk out of an air-conditioned building. Nicholas is thrilled to be at the pool where he can dig in the dirt in the corner by the hose. The fact that there is a large box of refreshing water filled with frolicking children and blow-up toys three feet behind his shoulder is of no consequence to him.

I sit on a pool chair waving beach props in the air in succession like I'm auctioning off valuables. I try to both respect his space in the corner by the hose and lure him to the pool water with colorful buckets, plastic watering cans, and a floating dinosaur dinghy. I finally let him be, deciding that this may be the lone summer that he hates the pool, the summer of folklore in a long string of water-logged summers where he will be the last kid out of the pool before the lifeguard jingles the lock and key at him from the front gate.

I spot a three-year-old girl in the water clutching her mother and screaming hysterically. Her mother asks her repeatedly to calm down, reminding her that she is safe. The girl's cries escalate. Despite her daughter's fear, the mother insists that she quiet down.

"*What* is the problem?" the mother asks as she lifts her daughter onto the concrete edge of the pool. "You know I would *never* let you go without telling you first," she adds. Sobbing, the little girl stretches her arms out to her mother.

"Calm down first, and then I'll hold you," the mother insists, which only makes the girl cry harder. The father comes over and holds his daughter, which stops her tears in an instant.

"I didn't *do* anything," insists the woman to her husband, shaking her head as she swims away. "She just started screaming for no reason. She should know that I would never let go of her."

When my son was a newborn, I took his tears so personally. Now that he is a toddler, I have at times taken his fears personally, too. Like his distress is a sign that I am doing something wrong as a parent. As if good parents have children with no fears whatsoever.

It's hard for us to allow our children to have their own perceptions, untainted and undefined by ours. I am beginning to realize that validation does not encourage a fear to linger or mushroom, but rather has the completely opposite effect. A validated fear seems to disappear. A validated need goes away. Respect for a child's perceptions, for his or her fears, is like balm.

I stare at the shallow end through that little girl's eyes, from my son's point of view, and suddenly three feet of water looks bottomless. The blue rectangle is an ocean. I feel unsafe even in the arms of my mother. I want the concrete edge, terra firma, under my feet. I want to play in the dirt in the corner by the hose. Just for this weekend. Just for this summer, the summer before I become a fish.

Humor me, Ma. Let me be irrationally fearful of deflating green balloons and lit birthday candles and car alarms going off in distant parking lots. I'll get over it. You might not believe me, but it's true. And I'm telling you, I won't remember a thing. I will have no recollection of Hoover terror or of my allergy to strollers, cars, crowds, baths, restaurants, and stethoscopes—I will only remember the way you made me feel about myself.

So don't worry, I'm not phobic or paranoid or weak—I'm just two. And hey, by the way, when are you gonna take me to the top of the Empire State Building?

CHAPTER SIXTEEN

Thank You, Beach

nder the gray shroud of a midday sky, the sand looks like a vast glacier of a beach, barren and long. There is not a soul in sight. My son and I are zipped to the chins, building cities out of buckets. He could care less that it's forty-eight degrees.

He is busy digging roads and boring tunnels, and I am lulled by his concentration, the sound of distant seagulls, and the smell of damp salty air.

"Varoooom!" he sings, moving mountains with his toy front-end loader.

Every ten minutes or so, he looks up at me and glances at the ocean waves playing tag with the pelicans, and he squeals, "Mahmee, we at da beach!" And he resumes his industrious sand-sculpting.

After an hour or so, I let him know it will be time to go in a few minutes. We begin to round up our tools and toys one by one. He puts his things in the plastic bag as I hold it open, calling them out in a checklist. I perch him on my left hip, and walk across the sand piles. Just as I lift my leg over the concrete embankment, he looks toward the ocean one more time.

"Fenk you, beach," he says softly.

My heart could scarcely contain the magnitude of his sentiment. For months now, I have been prompting him to parrot lines of gratitude to a neighbor for a cookie, a relative for a birthday gift, to people he doesn't even know for objects exchanged from their palm to his, and here he is thanking two miles of sand and the Atlantic Ocean.

He thanked the *beach*? Have *I* ever thanked the beach? Have I ever even thought to be even the slightest bit grateful to the beach?

How many other moments in my life have I experienced, taken, or consumed for my benefit, never thinking twice about being thankful not just *for* the experience, but *to* it? Thanking life for the very act of simply being in it. Isn't this the very essence of the spirit? Seeing the world—the beach—as something connected to us, and understanding that we are somehow changed in our relationship with it *because* of it?

He's almost two, and he is already one with the universe.

Our neighbor Catherine rings our doorbell with her usual offerings: homemade coconut cookies, ripe mangoes, rice pudding. Her kitchen looks like the outdoor markets of her native Bombay, wicker baskets on the floor filled with potatoes, onions, garlic, peppers. She cooks with her front door ajar, which means anyone within a hundred-foot radius is lucky enough to catch a whiff of her curried beef stew. I can't see her from our adjacent balcony, but through our screen doors I can hear her culinary rhythms, the way she taps her stirring spoon on the rim of her pot four times and bangs her pan on the element to stir sauce, while she hums to the strains of sitar music.

"Ni-co-leeee!" she yodels from her kitchen.

Nicholas and I head to the sliding door facing her front porch.

"Caff-rinnn!" he yells back, giggling.

"Ni-co-lee, I have something for you! I'm coming up."

Thirty seconds later, she stands on our welcome mat, wearing her apron and a sly grin.

"Ni-co-lee, for you." She extends her hand, balancing a single yellow pear on her open palm.

Nicholas gasps and reaches for it with a look of wonder, as if he is about to touch a rainbow.

"Thank you so much, Catherine!" I gush.

"You wehcome," chimes Nicholas.

"We say thank you to *Catherine,* honey," I clarify.

"Fenk you for da honey, Caff-rinn," he says.

Something about his unspoken reaction revealed more gratitude than any words he could parrot. It's like staring at the inside of the Sistine Chapel and saying, "Neat."

Do I want him to feel grateful or obliged? We tend to think of gratitude within the narrow confines of etiquette, but I see now that it has little to do with manners. Maybe gratitude is not so much about teaching a child to *be* thankful as it is about teaching him to *feel* thankful. Can it be taught or mirrored? Can I demonstrate instead of dictating?

If *I* feel grateful, then perhaps my son will feel my gratitude. And if I feel deprived, resentful, frustrated, indifferent? How would he find his way to a grateful heart if the people around him carried a list of grievances? He doesn't stand a chance of nurturing a spirit of appreciation if we were to walk with envy and longing.

If he is grateful to the beach, it's because he senses that it gave him something intangible. Joy? The chance to dream? The room to be himself? The space to explore without curtailing his curiosity?

It dawns on me that he has actually thanked me for all kinds of other unconventional events that I had acknowledged in the moment but dismissed in my mind. Tucking him in. Cutting his sandwiches in triangles. Wrapping him like a chrysalis in an extra large bath towel. Putting planet decals on his bedroom window. Sharing my ice cream cone after he has finished his own. Drawing pictures of fire trucks with his favorite green crayons. Kissing his scrapes. Holding him after a bad dream.

Dave and I have made a habit of thanking each other and Nicholas for the smallest of gestures, the most inconsequential of acts. Thanks for your company. For happy-face pancakes. For fun time at the zoo. For making music with me. For being there.

If a toddler can thank a beach for its gift, for what—not just to whom—do *I* feel thankful?

Beach gratitude has compelled me to take stock, do a sort of Inventory of Appreciation. To find magic in the mundane. To know what makes my life worth living. To remind myself always of the patchwork quilt that is life, each square a moment, a lesson, a prize, a gift.

I savor the memory of my beloved grandmother's cooking, her humor, her original hand-knit sweaters in lavender and fuchsia, her wisdom and aphorisms, the way she slipped wool socks on our cold feet even after we turned twenty-one. I try to fill her loss with love. To notice the details. I breathe in the scent of fresh basil. I bake chocolate chip cookies and eat them over the kitchen sink with Nicholas, both of us gulping cold milk in unison. Neither of us breathing a word of our appreciation because no words are necessary. I huddle under a street awning in a downpour and forget that I have no umbrella. I sit at the beach in my parka thankful, so thankful, for a fleeting moment.

Dinner's ready. A platter of chicken, rice, and sweet-potato fries sits in the middle of our round wooden table, steam rising to the ceiling lamp. The three of us hold hands before our meal. Over time, Nicholas begins to improvise, riffing on grace, as it were, and soon he is giving thanks for trucks. For chocolate sprinkles. For the photos my brother, Greg, sent him of his local fire station's shiny red fleet, and the cassette of the Manhattan Transfer singing "Trickle Trickle." For my sister Nora's rainbow Slinky, her handmade lollipop tree, and the neon stars for his bedroom ceiling. For my dad's cardboard cutout of the Lincoln Tunnel just big enough for his toy vehicles. For the chance to feed Topper a dog biscuit with Grandma Joan by his side. For building a wooden birdfeeder with his father and *his* dad, Grandpa Don.

Grace and gratitude. How much can he digest?

One evening at dinner, Nicholas wants to say a "diffrint grace." We wait curiously, Dave and I clasping hands with our boy in a triangle of extended limbs across the table. He takes a breath and says, "Dee God, uh . . . fenk you. Ahh-men."

And I think, Well, that just about sums it up now, doesn't it?

From infancy, we are taught to make wishes. Birthday candles, chicken wishbones, shooting stars, pennies in fountains, blow-away dandelions. Maybe we get used to thinking of that distant thing. Wishing feeds yearning, and before we know it, we don't recall where we are and how we got here, only that we want to be somewhere else. It's hard to feel grateful for a hole in our heart and a restlessness that spreads through our lives like an oil spill.

Once in a while, I forget to be happy. I forget the healing properties of gratitude, the power of suggestion, and the laws of physics. The apple does not fall far from the tree. Every action has an equal and opposite reaction.

CHAPTER SEVENTEEN

The Terribly Polite Twos

t's a bee-oo-tiful mornink!" Nicholas announces on our porch, his arms open wide like he's trying to hug the day. He sits on my left hip as I lock the front door.

Suddenly, he squeals, winds up, and socks me in the jaw. I am so startled from the pain that I drop everything on the front stoop, including him.

"*Ow!*" I howl. He looks at me in astonishment.

Later, I buckle him in the car seat after a fun afternoon together, and he coos, "Mommy! I wanna give you a big hug!" He wraps his little arms around my neck, and I melt like putty in the noonday sun. Then he yanks my braids as if they were parachute ripcords.

"Ouch!" I yelp. He begins to giggle.

"Dat is e-nuf!" he says to me earnestly.

I drive home in silence, wondering if I am a good mother, if he is going to take me for a ride even though I'm behind the wheel. I eye him in my rearview mirror, while he sings, "You gotta have hea-a-art . . . All ya really ne-e-ed is heart," and waves hello to every oil tanker that passes by.

Maybe *this* is what they mean by the terrible twos, I think. Isn't this the behavior that gets a parent's back up, arouses our darkest fears? Is this the early sign of a checkered life? Detentions? Running with "bad" crowds?

It's frighteningly easy to assume he's making a fool out of me. It amazes me that a creature of thirty-seven inches could render me so helpless. I'm not talking about his high-decibel resistance to a diaper change, or the way he goes limp noodle on me when I try to pick him up, or even his occasional disdain for civilian clothing. I'm talking about the torrent of feelings coursing through me when he looks me right in the eye and smirks like he is not only defying me, but mocking me at the same time. Like a heckler to a stand-up comic.

I know he is too young to understand mockery. He can't even blow his own nose.

Last weekend, my husband and I decide to take a family drive just after lunch. We head to a craft fair about sixty miles away in a quaint town on the New Jersey shore. Dave and I are sure our boy will sleep the whole ride.

But instead, on this afternoon, Nicholas sings every song he knows at the top of his lungs, blows four hundred and twelve raspberries until the front of his shirt is soaked, and thumps the back of my seat with his shoe to the rhythm of "Sweet Georgia Brown" as if this were something I might thoroughly enjoy.

Once we arrive, he wants to run for miles. He attempts to massage the wooden ornaments, sample miniature burbling pebble fountains, examine bonsai trees, and strum an electric guitar perched on its stand while the craft-fair band takes a coffee break. Dave and I are like linemen blocking for a bantam quarterback. Nicholas does some kind of Irish jig around a tent pole as the wind chimes shake and the merchants grab their craft tables as if a hurricane is about to blow through. His cheeks are flushed with heat and adrenaline and joyful abandon, his head full of chestnut curls bouncing with each step. Once he has done a lap or two of the grounds and assessed the situation, he mellows out, and Dave and I have a lovely time fulfilling our pregnant fantasies of meandering through country fairs on a sunny afternoon and buying a painted front end–loader lamp for our toddler's night table.

After the fair, we head six miles to the beach for dinner with friends before we drive home. At 6 p.m., we are the only people in the restaurant.

"Fenk yo-o-u-u!" chimes Nicholas as the waiter places the bread basket on our table.

We beam with pride at our son's impeccable manners. Suddenly, he throws his head back excitedly and tries out his new shrill scream.

"That is too loud, Nicholas," whispers Dave. "We use our indoor voice in the restaurant."

Nicholas laughs and yowls again.

"The restaurant does not allow screaming," I pronounce. "We don't want to startle the other people while they are eating."

He does his best imitation of a fire engine on an emergency rescue mission.

"Nicholas, *no* fire engines in the restaurant. Stop right now," says Dave.

"Whoo! Wee-ahh, wee-ahh!"

We try distraction. Storytelling. I Spy. He quiets down for fifteen minutes. Then, halfway through dinner, he begins an encore performance, this time to a full restaurant. He screeches again with a mouthful of spinach and mashed potato.

"That is enough!" I say sternly.

He flashes me this horrible adolescent look, as if to say I never did a thing for him in his whole life.

A well-dressed, middle-aged woman has been staring at me and my son, watching our small family drama unfold from her chair six feet away.

"How old is he?" she inquires.

I feel naked.

"He just turned two a couple months ago," I answer.

"Is he a good two or a bad two?" she asks.

"What do you mean?"

"Well, does he throw himself onto the mall floor and kick and scream? Does he have fits every time you want him to do something he doesn't want? Does he give you a hard time over meals, clothes, toys? You know, a bad two. *She* was a bad two," she says, pointing to her twelve-year-old daughter. "We spent most of our time disciplining her, spanking her for disobeying us. She always wanted to get her way. Her favorite word was no."

I glance at the girl while her mother talks about her as if she were not sitting right there eating tidy twisted forkfuls of linguine.

"No mall tantrums so far. No fits," I reply. "Actually, he doesn't say no that much."

I feel a hot ball of indignation in my gut.

No. One tiny word packs a lot of baggage.

Two little letters dredge up our own childhood misunderstandings, frustrations, limitations, vulnerability, misdemeanors, punishment, innocence, guilt. Suddenly, we have become our own parents. Our child has become the child in us, and we want to pull in the reins and release them at the same time.

It makes me wonder what we really want from our children. Do we secretly want whatever makes us feel comfortable, what makes us look good to other parents? Good manners. Obedience. Manageable energy levels.

When my son behaves cooperatively, politely, I feel I've got more than enough fuel for the ride. It's when he whines at me to make him something *else* for dinner after I've sliced, diced, layered, baked, and served lasagna that I feel inclined to toss the bowl of grated mozzarella in the air and escape through the chimney. During those blinding moments, I mistakenly see him as rude, ungrateful, selfish, and I feel the stakes go up a hundredfold. This is when a mother can tend to "lose it" because she feels her maternal efforts have been squandered. All that work for *this*?

I suppose it depends on which hot buttons are pressed in whom—and by whom. One toddler's curiosity is another's mischief. At least through the eyes of two different mothers. Maybe the mother whose own parent rejected her may perceive her own child's typical toddler defiance as an outright betrayal. Or a suspicious parent might tend to think a child is up to no good.

My son and his little playmate turn a deaf ear to me, and suddenly, I am ten, standing in my parents' backyard with a head full of blue Velcro trying to flatten my frizzy hair to look more like Eleanor and Leslie and Debbie from the Land of Straight-Haired girls. Scotty spots me through the shrubs and gathers enough ammunition for three days of school taunting.

"Hanassafrass wears curlers! Hanassafra-a-ass wears curlers!"

Decades later, I project my buried wounds, perceived injustices, once inflicted from one small heart to another. But it isn't my son's story. It isn't even mine anymore. Nicholas is not Scotty, and I like my curly hair just fine now.

It's easy to set up camps. Battle lines. It's easy to fall into the trap of perceiving a toddler's repeated "bad" behavior as antagonism and rebellion and the testing of only *our* limits and not his own.

Power. He wants it. Dave and I want it. We get anxious when we think he has it and we don't. Then I wonder if this is really about power at all.

What if I could see that my two-year-old was behaving appropriately for his age? After all, he does struggle with your garden-variety transition, the standard coming and going, not to mention loose socks, a spot of water on his shirt, and sticky fingers. So is it realistic for me to expect a giddy, overtired, overstimulated two-year-old to sit quietly for dinner in a crowded, bustling restaurant at 6 p.m. when he hasn't napped all day?

Does seeing things through his eyes mean I'm indulging him, encouraging him to become a person who expects the world to dote on him and answer his whims? Or does it let him know I accept him despite his passing quirkiness, at the same time that I'm setting firm boundaries?

Sometimes, I have to remind myself that I'm the grown-up. I can lose sight of the fact that my son isn't here to thwart me, override me, or get me out of his way. If I cannot understand that he needs me in his way as much as he needs to find his own, then I leave the door wide open to misunderstandings, misperceptions, and mutiny.

If I experience the world from just above the knee, I see that, at two, my son isn't the least bit worried about what others may think of him, as I might be. I really can't expect him to conform to all norms and rules at once, especially the ones that he cannot yet grasp. He hasn't yet fully gotten the notion that walking in the street might be fatal. How could he comprehend the unwritten social law that says we ought to respect each other's right to a quiet meal?

At times like these, I wonder how many of our expectations of our own child are shaped by the expectations of others. I recall that earlier a harried woman was attempting to enter the restaurant with her child in a stroller, struggling with the door and the wheels of her buggy, *so sorry* for all the trouble. Sorry for blocking the way. Sorry the doors aren't made for mothers pushing strollers. Sorry strollers are so big and clumsy. Sorry for the inconvenience. Sorry my toddler is screaming in the restaurant with a mouthful of food. Sorry he's disturbing your meal.

That woman, of course, was me. Dave was parking the car on a side street while I went ahead to get us a table.

There is our perception of our child. There is society's view. And there is our reaction to society's view. Is it embarrassment, outrage, indifference, defensiveness? Or a simple acknowledgment that there is a world out there with a certain protocol, and that in due time, our children will have to know how to stand in single file and walk to fire exits like everyone else?

As a parent, I have to be willing to test my own limits, reevaluate my own expectations and ideas. It's about relationship. What am *I* doing? How am I contributing to this situation? Is my child reacting to something I am doing or not doing? I have to look at myself. No guilt. No blame. Just honest self-examination.

"Stop talking, Mommy," my son says to me one afternoon, interrupting one of my cogent lectures on early childhood development, "Why We Do Not Drop Crayons into the Floor Heaters."

A mother of four children I met at a toddler gymnastics class had an interesting take on how much small children really understand. She explained that her son seems to grasp very complex concepts yet is baffled by relatively simple ones. She said that sometimes when she's talking to him about inappropriate behavior, he begins to respond in a kind of gibberish. Instead of seeing what she called his nonsense talk as rude or silly, she perceives it as his way of telling her that he's confused. He reverts to a "language he knows best."

That rings a bell. For the record, here's the rest of my floor-heater dissertation: "Nicholas, we *never* put anything in the floor heaters, not crayons, not sand, not your toothbrush. Heaters have to stay clean and clear so the heat can come out. If they get blocked, it can be dangerous. We *stay away* from the floor heaters."

He stares right into my eyes as I speak, following, I presume, every nuance of my speech.

"What's de white part of yer eye called?" he asks, still gazing at my face.

"The cornea," I reply. "Did you hear what I said about the floor heaters?"

"What's de color part?"

"The iris," I sigh. "Don't touch the floor heaters."

"What's de black dot in da middo?"

"The pupil."

"I haff ah idea!" he shrieks. "We cin make gingerbread cookies an' put white choc-lit chips for de cornea and black ones for de puppel!"

Eureka. (Note: He never touched the floor heaters again.)

Since Nicholas started talking when he was ten months old, I have often had to remind myself that he is still in diapers. I realize that the words that come out of his mouth belie his age. But his vocabulary really isn't the point. (Einstein didn't start talking until after he was three.) His knack for conversation has helped me understand him in a way that makes me wonder what I would think of his actions if he couldn't say, "Mah-mee! I'm chopping wood!" while loudly banging his spoon on his tray table. It compels me to want to give a child the benefit of the doubt whether or not he has the words to express his needs or his intentions.

Sometimes, I think he's a boy genius. And then, some days I see how much he has in common with a small puppy.

One day, he falls off a chair in a restaurant and cuts his lower lip on the edge of the wooden table. Blood in the sink, tears, pain, trauma. That same afternoon, he sits on a chair at home and tips it precariously forward in exactly the same way. Is that defiance? Is he trying to hurt himself again?

I think about the things I say to him. When he's standing on his dump truck and I tell him he's going to break it, maybe he hears that as a missive to do so.

I try different responses.

On our way to the driveway one afternoon, he takes a detour and bolts across the lawn toward the street. He stops and looks around for me by the bushes. When I approach him, he smiles at me and says, "Dat's unacceptabo!"

I want to roll on the grass and howl with laughter, but instead I agree with him. He looks extremely pleased with himself while walking a straight line to the car.

I have a lightbulb moment.

I can actually allow him to test me without making it about me. I can see his testing of me as normal, even necessary. I can see his testing of me as a testing of himself. It means that I stop polarizing issues in my mind as His Way versus My Way.

Yes, I have to remember all of this the next time I order him to stop playing the piano with the spatula.

I realize the myth of one-time discipline. Freud said that repetition is the mother of invention. But most days, I feel more like repetition is the invention of mothers.

Nicholas is in the middle of a fevered drum solo on metal mixing bowls. I clap along with his rhythm. He beams, then suddenly bops me on the head with his wooden spoon and does a cymbal crash on my left shoulder.

"That hurt!" I shriek.

I get the distinct feeling that the way I handle his behavior could actually determine the course it takes. The way I perceive his behavior, the way I react, the words I use to describe his actions and my feelings could either encourage it to continue, exacerbate it, turn it into a pattern, or stop it without incident.

The next time he pinches me, I say firmly, "I don't like that." I try telling him to be gentle. But I am increasingly unsettled with the words. Urging him to be gentle assumes that he is being aggressive. Is he? The question begs my reconsideration. I see that every time he seems to act "aggressively," it's in the context of play.

If we were to tell him to be gentle five, twenty, a hundred times a day, wouldn't we indirectly be telling him he isn't? Wouldn't he then get the repeated message that he is an aggressive person? That aggressive is negative, bad? That *he* is bad? And might we not be setting him up to fulfill that perception?

I wonder if, in asking him to be gentle, I might be assigning the wrong motivation to his gesture, reacting to him as if his *intention* were borne of malice instead of enthusiasm. I'd be labeling him hostile when he might have only been excited. I would be telling him he was something he wasn't. What kind of confusion might I be sowing in his mind by chastising him for being mean when his kindness is not even the issue?

If he had pulled my braids at nine months old, the last thing I'd have thought of was his aggression, his defiance, his power play. So why am I so willing to assume something different about his character just because he's a toddler?

The next time he pulls my locks, tweaks my cheek, plays my thigh like a bongo, I say, "Nicholas, I know you're very excited right now. And I know you don't want to hurt Mommy, but that was too hard. See my arm?"

He stops cold, gazes at the red blotch with great concern, then leans forward to kiss it.

"Is dat better now, Mommy?" he asks.

I notice that the more I give him a say, the more he listens. The more I empathize with his frustrations, the less he tends to hold on to them. The more I focus on the emotion behind his outburst, the shorter his meltdown. The more I identify with him, the more he cooperates and respects the limits I set for him. The more I see him within the context of our relationship, I see that the relationship itself is what shapes him, not my parental righteousness.

It keeps me honest.

I don't want him to be a blank slate upon which others might write his story. I want him to have the courage to stand his ground. Even if he is only two.

And when he can't have his way, I want to teach him humility instead of humiliation. I want to teach him how to cope instead of scolding him for losing control. I want to give him the benefit of the doubt, the right to change his mind without ridiculing him for being fickle. I want to teach him empathy instead of shame.

I can see that his refusals and protests are not a sign of his rudeness, ingratitude, or rejection of me. He is trying his little self on for size. Nothing personal. His right to say no is also his rite.

Dave and Nicholas left the restaurant twenty minutes ago to watch the sunset from the boardwalk by the beach across the road. I sit at the table picking at the rest of my now cold dinner. The fresh evening air has surely calmed Nicholas down. When I join them, I am expecting to see our son asleep on his father's shoulder, little limbs dangling like a marionette. Instead, I find Dave standing, shoulders slouched, with sand in his hair. His silver wire-rim glasses are crooked. Nicholas is running up and down the boardwalk, his knees buckling with fatigue every time he slows down to tag Dave.

"You're it!" he giggles.

"A holy terror," Dave mumbles to me slowly, his eyebrows raised.

"That's an awful thing to say!" I whisper. "I'm going to get him washed up in the restaurant bathroom before we leave."

I put him in the stroller and begin to walk briskly toward the crosswalk. My mind is reeling. *Is* our son a threat to our equilibrium? Does his energy push us past a reasonable limit? What is a reasonable limit? My heart is racing.

Is our very balance at stake? I wonder.

Just then, the stroller's front wheels hit a three-inch rise in the asphalt, and the stroller, Nicholas, and I flip over in the middle of the intersection. I land on my elbow. Nicholas, thankfully, is shielded by the diaper bag that flung over from the handlebars. I crawl under the bag and find him sitting strapped in his stroller upside down, his hands folded neatly in his lap.

"What happened?" he asks softly.

Shaken from the fall, I take a deep breath and brush the gravel from my bloody elbow.

"We're okay, honey," I say, reassuring both of us. "It's getting late and we're all tired. It's time to head home.

CHAPTER EIGHTEEN

The Son Also Rises

y husband and I, fast asleep a split second ago, fling the covers off and bounce off our mattress from opposite sides, as if our bed was suddenly infested with scorpions. I glance at the neon-red numbers on my nightstand. 3:37 a.m.

Nicholas's scream explodes into the night air like a hand grenade. Dave and I sprint to his bedside in four giant strides.

"What's the matter, sweetie?"

He is weeping uncontrollably, a mournful wail with long, slow phrases.

"Nicholas, honey, Mommy and Daddy are here. You're safe."

He sits by the wall on crumpled bedsheets, head bowed, his hands in his lap.

"Did you have a bad dream?"

He nods with eyes closed and retrieves an image.

"My bed . . . was a tugboat . . . an da sail fell off."

Maybe the stroller flip the other day traumatized him. I don't know. What I do know is that one year after the waking baby finally got it together overnight, twelve months after the sleep-deprived mother finally stopped wearing concealer to bed, the son rises once again.

My face is not at all pleased about this. Just ask my chin, which has recently begun migrating south. When Nicholas does sleep from nine to six, I wake up with all my features intact, with eyes, nose, and mouth in the same time zone, a nice bonus that can make a woman feel pretty darn good about herself.

The older a baby gets, the more we expect sleep to be a nonissue. Nobody asks if the two-year-old is sleeping the night. They assume he does. And to those inquiring, I say, "He can. He did. He will again."

And yet, gather a group of twenty mothers with toddlers, and you'll hear variations on the same theme. Nightmares. Night terrors. Unexplained waking, crying, pleading for company and a glass of water.

What is going on? What kind of cruel phenomenon is this? Is this a symptom of some hideous sleep disorder? A sign of toddler insanity? A foreshadowing of our own?

Here's my theory: small people are growing. Yes, synapses are firing. Little heads are swirling with images and fears of a world that is looking bigger every day. A child wanders through the day, absorbing, digesting, analyzing, and deciphering words, explanations, grimaces, transactions, the emotional landscape of those around him. He's all eyes and ears, looking at and listening to the world and figuring out where he fits into it. I take note as my son unwittingly tells me what piques his curiosity, what frightens him, what makes him happy, what confuses him, and, if he has any inkling, why. Sometimes, I don't completely know the answers until he has confirmed them at 3:04 a.m.

Strangely, groggily, temporarily, it's all part of the process of getting to know him.

"Can't do it!" he cries out at 3 a.m.

"Do what, Nicholas?" I ask, half-asleep.

"A somasault . . . ," he replies, dazed. Clearly, he has a lot on his mind.

Like all young children, he is highly impressionable. At the beach, he walks over to an older boy's sandcastle to get in on the action.

"Ta-DA!" Nicholas screams with joy.

The boy is so annoyed that he barks, "Hey! What are you doing?"

Nicholas doesn't flinch at the volume or the boy's outright rejection. But a week after we get home from our trip, he wakes up in the middle of the night and yells, "Hey! What are you *doing*?" When I approach him, he is standing in the dark, blinking at his mattress and the sandcastle ruins around his feet.

In the grocery store, a woman comes barreling down the aisle with her cart and stops an inch from Nicholas's face.

"Ex-*cuse* me!" says Nicholas emphatically.

"Oh, I'm sorry!" says the lady. "I was going too fast!"

This four-and-a-half-second conversation between a highly caffeinated woman and a startled toddler is repeated in an endless loop in the weeks, even months, that follow. He is perfectly silent, concentrating on a book or crayon drawing, when he says under his breath, "Da lady say, 'Oh, I'm sorry, I was going too fast.'" Then he improvises, riffing on the main theme. "I was going too fast with dat zooming grocery cart." The story wends its way into his dreams, so that it isn't clear anymore which is reality and which is fantasy.

One afternoon, he inadvertently pokes a hole in our front screen door with the small knob on his toy truck.

"Da truck broke da screen . . . ," he says softly, with amazement and remorse.

He returns to the hole many times in the days to come. Leans into it. Inspects it closely. Sniffs it. Lightly rubs his finger over it.

Stares at it for long silent minutes. This makes for excellent wakeup fodder. Sure enough, one morning at 4 a.m., he says slowly, "Mahmee . . . dat truck . . . broke . . . da screen." I acknowledge the fact, and let him know that it's okay, that the screen and the truck are both sleeping now.

"It made a hole," he murmurs, with his eyes closed.

It isn't always an event that makes its imprint on his unconscious mind. A couple of nights in a row, Nicholas has woken because his socks were apparently sliding off. He lies down while I pull them back up.

"Tighter," he mumbles, half-asleep.

And sometimes, it's a new word. One night, he breaks the wee-hour silence with a loud "Suddenly," and then doesn't utter a word until 7 a.m.

Another night, the local fire department dispatches its fleet of pumper trucks and squad cars on a ten-mile caravan with sirens blaring, and Nicholas wakes up prepared to go outside in his pajamas and follow them barefoot. And I remind him that it's dark, that when it's dark we sleep, that he understands, right?

"You undastand, Mahmee."

Well before dawn, Nicholas makes some odd guttural noise that summons me to his crib, where he looks at me plain as day and says, "We bofe haff noses." I have never wanted to laugh so hard at 4 a.m.

The most bizarre: "Mahmee, da Menorrah is in da window at da bank!"

And the most flattering: "Mah-mee, you a cutie."

Horror stories abound. Coat hangers lodged in the door to prevent children from exiting their rooms after bedtime. Hooks and eyes outside the door to lock them in. Serious threats of not crossing the threshold of the room for any reason whatsoever. And these are accounts from college-educated professionals, parents who would never want any harm to come to their children. They just believe that night-waking is bad behavior.

But is this a discipline issue? Should our children be more independent at two, even though it says "dependent" on our tax forms?

My girlfriend Ludivine remembers how she used to stroke her mother's earlobe to fall asleep when she was little. She tells me this as she tugs on her own earlobe twenty-five years later.

Another friend, Lana, finds her son Reese's face nuzzled into the back of her hair every morning, snoring like it's midnight. He gets out of bed sometime during the night and knows what he needs and where he'll find it.

"It's comfort," she says. "That deep sense of security. Sure, I'm sleep-deprived. In fact, with my two boys, I haven't slept the night in eight years. But, you know what? My youngest won't be snuggling in our bed when he's twelve. So for now, if this is what he needs, I say, fine, come on in."

"Nip that in the bud," warns another mother, "because before you know it, they're asking for this or that. They'll know exactly how to maneuver you so they get it."

But this is not manipulation. It's a seven-year-old boy who goes to his grandma's funeral and can't sleep for months afterward because he's afraid of what might happen to him in the dark. It's the four-year-old who cuddles up with his mother every night because she is ill and he wants to wrap his arms around her and never let go. It's the girl who started school and feels the pangs of separation. The two-year-old who dreams of caterpillars in his bed. The child who is caught in the crosshairs of divorce. And the one who didn't get enough time during the day with a working parent.

Simply, it's the child who wants to cozy up with the people he or she loves.

There's a lot to contend with when you're small. Potty training.

Eating with your own fork. Leaving mother in small increments daily. The pull of autonomy and the simultaneous tug of dependence. The growing pressures to conform, to share, to be polite, to control one's frustration, to be less clingy, less shy, more self-sufficient. The pressure to be one way and not another—to be, perhaps, a way that feels contrary to a child's natural impulses. Growing must sometimes feel overwhelming to pint-sized sensibilities.

How do we respond to a child's nocturnal request for reassurance?

My friend Leslie came up with an ingenious way of dealing with her daughter's repeated nightmares and subsequent fear of going to sleep. Every night after she and her husband Jamie read bedtime stories with their daughter, Alanna, they asked her to dip her hand into a glass container filled with little folded pieces of white paper, and fish one out. Inside each note were a few words that described something she loved. Pony rides. Making ice cream sundaes. Chasing the tide. Picking apples from a tree. Each night, after reading one message, they would turn off the light and whisper in the dark for a minute, setting the scene so Alanna could take it with her to sleep and finish the story in her dreams. This worked for her in a way that an hour of verbal reassurance could never have. She needed a parent to crawl inside the cramped quarters of her sleepless night and think. Think with her. Think *like* her.

There's something about the night. Poets have written about it for centuries. The lure of the dark, the sweet promise of sleep, the antidote for overwrought limbs and a troubled spirit, the little death that is surrender.

Who knows how a child perceives his night-waking? Maybe to him it's wrapped up in separation anxiety. Or in our own anxious push for our child's early independence. Or in the birth of a sibling. How do we feel if our child needs us at a time when we think he ought to need us *less*? Do we allow him to seek us out or persuade him to turn away from us?

I'm willing to bet the farm that the snuggles don't foster apathy. Love doesn't breed chaos. Comfort won't teach deceit. Security will not stoke insecurity.

Any way we do the math, our children won't be waking up looking for us fifteen years from now. That's because (1) they'll have grown out of it, and (2) *we* will be waking up looking for *them*.

It's bedtime. My son nestles into my arms and sighs, "Cozee, cozee," and closes his eyes. He pats my cheek and says, slurring his words, "Dath yer Mah-mee."

A few minutes later, he is near slumber when he shouts in a loud whisper, "Goodnight moon!" as if he just realized he left his wallet in a taxi after it sped away. He attempts to get up, but I pull him back gently and explain that we are going to sleep now.

"Mah-mee, read *Goodnight Moon.* Would like to read it! Great ideeah!"

I meet him halfway. We lie in the shadows, and I whisper an abridged version of the book, to the best of my memory. He hangs on every syllable and drifts off within three minutes. He sleeps the whole night.

Maybe it was the salmon and rice he had for dinner.

At 5:05 a.m., I'm dreaming of a choir. Then, it dawns on me that I am actually awake and my two-year-old is singing "Hallelujah" sotto voce.

"Ha-lay-you-ya . . . ha-lay-you-ya."

I'm not even sure his eyes are open.

By 5:09 a.m., silence. After a short Christmas medley in the middle of April, he serenades himself back to sleep until eight-thirty.

CHAPTER NINETEEN

Sandbox Politics

y son and I dig for oil. We are in the neighborhood sandbox along with six other toddlers.

"A je-e-ep," he whispers rapturously, spotting a toy in another child's hand.

"Share, Justin!" calls out a woman from the shaded bench under the maple tree.

Justin looks like something out of Oliver Twist, his lips turned down at the edges, hair and clothes tousled, his eyes dark and brooding.

"Give the boy that jeep!" the mother orders.

"It's okay," I call over to her, following Nicholas to the swings.

"No," she argues. "It's not okay. He has to share!"

The boy squints at my son perched in his bucket swing by the wire-mesh fence; then he glances back down at the dusty dune buggy in his hand. There are no other children in the box now. He is sitting alone on his calves in the sand.

"Drop it!" barks his mother, like a narcotics cop. I half expect her to pull out a megaphone and start yelling, *Step away from the jeep, and put your hands in the air!* Justin glances at his toy one last time, looks around, blinks a few times, slowly places the car a few inches to his left on the sand. Then he stares off into the distance.

A few weeks later, Nicholas and I head to a park in New Jersey by the Hudson River, a fenced-in park with a view of Manhattan, surrounded by American flags and lots of goose poop. I lug a big plastic bag as we approach the sandbox filled with children, sit on the wooden ledge, and one by one unload the dump truck, steamroller, front-end loader, bucket, sifter, shovel, and pail.

"Would anyone like to play with us?" I ask.

Some children begin to walk over, eyeing their parents for approval; others sit still, wondering if this might be a nefarious kidnapping plot.

Nicholas, gripping a large yellow front-end loader in his left hand, spots the exact same toy in the hands of a boy in the sandbox, walks over with his arm extended, and grabs it from him, exhibiting the Universal Toddler Law of Attraction to Other Children's Stuff. The boy begins to cry. I walk over to my son, crouch down to his ear level, and explain that we don't grab, that grabbing hurts the boy's feelings, that we need to ask the boy if he wants to share, and that if he says yes, *then* we can take it and say thank you. Nicholas lets go of the boy's front-end loader, and I feel a deep sense of satisfaction that he has understood the simple dynamics of sharing.

I might as well have been explaining the square root of a tuna sandwich.

"A tiny little yellow e-xcava-ator!" Nicholas swoons, spotting a toy in the hands of an older toddler in the sand. "Fenk you!" my son says as he reaches out and wraps his fingers around it.

"It's mine!" screams the three-year-old boy.

I sit just outside the sandbox watching this scene, realizing that my son has evidently not understood, and may have just filed the boy's reaction in the back of his mind under Intriguing Things I've Seen Other Children Do.

"Nicholas, the little boy is busy playing with it now," I say, resorting to the fine art of distraction. "Why don't we make sandcastles with all these buckets?"

Instead, with nine plastic pails overturned in a cluster, Nicholas begins to tap the bottoms with his palms.

The boy drops his toy, and wanders over to our sandbox rhythm section. I gather up some twigs and distribute the drumsticks, and we all make music while the toppled yellow excavator lies half buried in the sand.

Days later, Dave, Nicholas, and I are on our way out of a pizzeria when we pass a table where a boy of about seven is playing with a small toy backhoe. Nicholas stops, and suddenly screams, "No, it's mine!" He then smiles and walks right by the boy, as if to wink and say, "Hey, pal, have a good night."

On a stormy afternoon, my son and I venture to the Children's Museum ten miles from our house. It's set up in an old warehouse in an industrial park. We enter the building, make a sharp right past the miniature train station and pint-sized space shuttle, and then head straight for the indoor sandbox. This one is filled with barefoot toddlers and dump trucks the size of small farm animals. A shiny museum artifact catches my son's eye, a lone toy fire engine in the sand, bigger than a click beetle, smaller than a yam. He settles into a love affair with the fire engine, whispering sweet nothings to its ladder, telling the vehicle how happy he is to see it today.

Enter Harrison, a three-year-old with monogrammed knit vest, cuffed pants, and brown hair parted on the left and neatly combed back.

"Hi," chirps Nicholas, "what's yer name?"

The boy stares and says nothing. Suddenly, he grabs the fire engine from Nicholas's hands and holds it above his head, while my son dances on his toes and swipes the air like a dog on hind legs begging for his biscuit.

"Harrison, share!" his mother instructs.

My attempts to distract either of them with other museum artifacts are futile. I explain to Nicholas that the boy doesn't want to play together today, and that I understand his frustration. I then remind both boys that the toy belongs to the museum so that all of the children can play with it. I might have been more effective discussing campaign finance reform.

On the way home in the car, the rain is pounding on our roof, and my son is unusually quiet. I eye him in the rearview mirror at the traffic light. He looks preoccupied. A two-year-old lost in thought. Breaking his silence, he says slowly, shaking his head, "I can't play wid dat fire engine . . ." He stares at the rain-streaked window. "Because . . . dat boy was . . . *sharing!*"

It occurs to me that if he heard the word "share" every time there was a squabble over a toy, it made some kind of curious toddler sense that he'd actually connect the two. Sharing and fighting. I begin to rethink the notion from a child's perspective, wondering about terminology and semantics, and a parent's take on sharing.

We are stopped at a traffic light sometime later, when Nicholas begins to get impatient.

"It's their turn to go right now, and our turn to wait," I say. "We're taking turns. Like the tennis players down the street from our house, taking turns hitting the ball back and forth to each other. Like the ice cream cone we took turns licking last week."

Just then, the light turns green, and Nicholas chirps, "Now it's our turn!" as if the light had just turned green in his head. That's it, I think. At least taking turns gives him a turn, unless of course the other person just isn't in the mood.

———

Several weeks later, it's a cloudless day at Goose Poop Park, and my son is instantly captivated by the sight of a yellow, red, and blue toy bulldozer in the hands of a three-year-old boy.

"I would like to play wid dat buh-dozer," my son says to him.

The boy frowns and hides it behind his back.

"He's playing with it, Nicholas. Maybe once the boy is finished, he might give you a turn. I'm sure you can find something else to play with right now," I suggest.

"Dat's a buh-dozer wid a red shovel, boy!" my two-year-old says, trying to break the ice with the three-year-old boy who ignores him.

"May I see dat buh-dozer please, boy?" asks Nicholas, while the boy huddles over it.

"Scuze me, boy," he asks again, circling him like a bear at a picnic. "May I please have dat buh-dozer?"

Boy growls and gently nudges Nicholas with his arm to move out of his space. My son doesn't get the message.

"Nicholas, he wants to play alone right now," I pipe in, noticing the boy's mounting anxiety.

"What's yer name?" my son asks, bending down sideways to peer under the brim of the boy's red sunhat at his face.

Ten minutes later, Nicholas picks up his own front-end loader, approaches the boy, and suggests, "You can play wid dis front-end loader," hoping for a clean swap. The boy gets up and runs behind the bench where his mother is seated. Nicholas follows, figuring he's now playing a game of hide-and-seek-the-bulldozer.

I gently and firmly reiterate to my son that the boy does not want to take turns right now, that we must respect his wishes. I try to redirect his attention and his body. I guide him to another spot in the box. To the swings. The slide.

My son is like a boomerang.

"Can I *please* have a turn wid dat buh-dozer?" Nicholas tries again, crowding the other child.

I notice a flash of something in the boy's eyes that disturbs me. I kneel in the sand next to Nicholas and tell him that although I know he tried very hard to convince him, the boy would rather not play today. Before I can say another word, the boy snarls and smacks my son on the cheek with his plastic shovel.

"No!" I bark sternly.

His mother walks over and mumbles something in his left ear. My son stands mutely staring at him, tears in his eyes. The boy and his mother say nothing to either of us. I feel a volcanic rage inside my chest. I suddenly hate that boy, hate his floppy red sunhat and dirty little fingernails and thin locked lips. Hate his mother, her crossed arms, her ancestors, her short cropped hair, and baby-blue toenail polish.

Nicholas whimpers and catches his breath.

"Dat boy . . . *hit* me," Nicholas mumbles in disbelief, his eyes fixed on him. Then he slowly leans forward and holds his palms over the boy's head. Just as I expect him to give the boy a retaliatory wallop, Nicholas lifts his hands briskly as if over a hot stove, and walks away.

I could have forced my son out of the sandbox a half hour earlier. I could have scooped him up and coerced him into a bucket swing on the other side of the park to avoid the confrontation. I could have removed him from the park entirely at the first sign of bulldozer obsession and driven elsewhere. And maybe I should have.

But, rather than avoiding the challenges of sharing, I guess I felt the importance of allowing my son the opportunity to try out his own diplomatic relations—to experiment with his own approach and negotiations, his bartering and trading—and let the outcome of those transactions unfold.

We make choices with our child's best interests in mind, yet I can't help but think about other children too. What about taking the shy one's best interests into consideration? Sometimes, the extroverted child can innocently and unwittingly ruin the day for the timid.

Who draws the line in the sand—the child or the parent?

Maybe I could have sensed that boy's anxiety in a way that would have compelled me to intervene and quietly remove my child from the box, not to avoid a confrontation but to be sensitive to another child's needs. Ultimately, a parent makes certain decisions in the moment, some of which we stand by and others which we may later regret.

I loathed the plastic-shovel smack to Nicholas's cheek, but I realized that somehow, in that one ugly moment, he might have begun to learn something important about other people's boundaries. He will have to learn about other people's limits. About his own.

And by my son's final gesture, I learned something about forgiveness.

Letting my two-year-old struggle to define sharing has forced me to redefine it. I've realized how difficult sharing is for small people because I see how difficult it is for adults. When an adult buys a new car, the last thing he wants to do is share it with anyone who wants to drive it. He doesn't want to hand over the keys any more than a child wants to hand over the dump truck.

Sharing is not a skill like learning to tie shoes. It's a process, not a one-time lesson.

Our sharing messages are laden with contradictions. We don't like our children to be possessive, yet we reinforce possessions, regularly reminding them of what's yours, his, or hers. We want our children to share their toys, but when they grow up, we tell them to hold on to their stuff.

We want our toddlers to be "nice," but when they're grown we tell them that nice people get walked on. We think nice children are lovable and nice adults are doormats.

We think not sharing is about not being nice, about being self-ish, about a lack of empathy for others, about an inability to get along with peers. To a child, not sharing is a choice depending on the toy, the time of day, his molars, whether he had a nap, too much juice, not enough attention, and forty-seven other possible contributing factors. Not wanting to share has nothing to do with our child's character or his future.

We say sharing is about giving, yet we teach it by demand. If we order it and our child follows our instruction, he is not giving but obeying. He shares to avoid our disapproval and punishment, not because he feels a sense of goodwill and compassion for his fellow toddler.

We expect our babies and toddlers to feel a sense of goodwill and compassion toward others when they still can't have their noses wiped without crying.

Instead of letting our children explore the opportunity to learn about group dynamics, their own impulses, other children's reactions, conflict, and resolution, we insist on an ultimatum approach to sharing. Share—or else.

We give our children the subtle message that the way to solve a conflict is to give in. We coax our children to share as a means of avoiding confrontation. We instruct them to share with everyone equally, instead of allowing them the freedom to be discerning, to make their own naive judgments about who they want to share with and who they don't connect with. We're afraid that would teach them prejudice.

We'd rather have a child obey our sharing orders and not have a clue why he is doing it, than have a child who doesn't want to hand over the truck and be perfectly clear about his motivations.

It's been a few months since the shovel smack incident. I let Nicholas do the recounting so I can understand how he perceived it, see whether he places the emphasis on the toy or the boy or the smack—or himself.

I don't want to rehash the incident, trusting instead that Nicholas remembers it and has processed it on some level. I don't want to warn him of future conflicts, because doing so might instill anxiety and deter him from approaching other children altogether. And I don't want to coach him on the necessity of self-restraint, because that might give him the message that conflicts are a result of *his* poor judgment or his enthusiasm, curiosity, and persistence.

About six weeks later, we're at a sandbox in Froggy Park, shaded by magnolia and pine trees. My son is busy pouring sand from one pail to another when a little boy walks over and sits down in front of him. The child studies him quietly. After about twenty seconds, Nicholas looks at him, hands him a shovel and a pail, and says, "Here, take a turn."

The two of them sit in the sand and play next to each other in silence. Later, Nicholas spots a small toy truck in the hands of another child in the sandbox. He walks over and asks, "Could I have a turn?" The boy says nothing. Nicholas asks again. "Can *I* play with dat truck?" The boy grunts and shakes his head. And this time, my son accepts the child's refusal and walks away.

A few months later, he is playing with a toy that another child wants. I ask Nicholas if he wants to offer the child a turn.

"No," he says, matter-of-factly.

"I guess you're not finished playing with it yet," I acknowledge. "Well, maybe when you're done, you can give him a turn."

Ten minutes later, Nicholas gets up on his own accord, walks over to the boy, and hands him the toy.

There are times when being in a group energizes a child, and times when he wants to play alone in or apart from a crowd. And there are those times when taking turns makes as much sense to him as eating boiled parsnips.

I now see how unnecessary our coaxing can sometimes be, how confusing it might sound to a small mind trying to process the dichotomy, and how clear it is that a child can feel the emotion of his own gestures. Does he really need me to assign an adjective, a value, to his every action? Does he not sense, on some level, that fighting feels uncomfortable—and that giving feels good?

Nicholas still thinks all toys are his, even if they are at somebody else's house. He still asks for a turn and takes it simultaneously. But I hope he is beginning to understand that life isn't the same every day, that different people have different responses, that their responses are not always about him, that asking doesn't always mean getting, that not getting doesn't mean he will never get again. That giving feels good not necessarily because he might get something in return.

Several months later, Nicholas and I are at Goose Poop Park with a stash of toy vehicles. He is lying on his right side in the sandbox following the motion of the wheels on his front-end loader, a red baseball cap shielding his eyes from the bright midday sun. I am on the bench reading when I see a boy walk toward him with a bag of toys. Nicholas jumps up to greet him.

"Hi, I'm Nicholas. Who're you?"

"Andy."

"Cin I play wit yer excavator?"

"Yes," the boy says smiling.

"Sure?" Nicholas squeals. "Dis is my wagon truck an' my tractor wit a plow an' my digger. You cin play wit dem!"

I watch as the two of them crouch into position like long-lost pals, their bellies on the sand and sandals in the air. I ought to get that boy's number and get them together for a playdate, I plot quietly. What a sweet little guy, so open, so willing, so eager to share and to connect. I gaze at his crop of sandy hair, cut in a tidy line across his forehead, his lively blue eyes and broad smile. Then I suddenly recognize him.

It's the boy.

Dat boy.

Dat boy wit da buhdozer.

CHAPTER TWENTY

Rocking My Baby Back Home

am in the back of a New York city cab. My friend Jane and I are stuck in midtown at rush hour. We kick off our shoes and stretch our legs, smearing our lipstick into tissues after being "on" all day in a television studio. How are the boys? What are they doing? What about dinner? Are you getting any sleep? What's happened to our bodies? How's the hubby? Thinking of having another baby?

"So, how do you surrender to your baby's needs without losing yourself?" I ask, half expecting her to laugh me right out of the taxi and into oncoming traffic.

Instead she looks at me square in the eye and says without skipping a beat, "Oh, I think you *do* lose yourself for the first few years. I think we're supposed to."

I think back to two years ago. How, with his sensitivities to light, sound, vibration, crowds, vacuums, bathwater, cars, and strollers, our newborn seemed to be lamenting, "I liked it better in there. Can't I go back . . . just for a little while longer?"

I assumed my fledgling position in the rocking chair to nurse, comfort, and console him. Somehow, through the chaos of those early months, he found his bliss. But there was a proviso. As long as

I held him close, rocking, walking, swaying, he was calm. I stood at the crossroads. How much should I give, and how much can I hold back? I didn't expect to find any answers in a rocking chair.

Two years have passed. It's early morning. Dave is still asleep. The sun is beginning to peek through the slats of the window blinds. Nicholas and I are tucked into the rocker in our flannel pajamas, his limbs still just small enough to fold into my lap. We rock, and I stare at the small head tucked into the nook of my left arm. My eyes follow the grain of his hair, the color of wheat and wet sand, swirling clockwise around his head. I fan out his toes in my hand like a deck of cards, studying the ones that look like mine (and my father's), the ancestral big toe that looks like my husband's (and his mother's).

Twelve minutes into the start of another day, and already my mind is in a jumble. Backandforthbackandforthbackandforth. We rock, and I coax my knots out of hiding, untying them with my eyes closed. I slow down and hear the layers of sound, faint and muffled, that I would otherwise think of as silence: the refrigerator fan whirring, water trickling down the pipes from the apartment upstairs, the delivery truck driving up the block, my own breath. Like dreaming in wild, lush colors while I'm wide awake.

When I glance at the clock, ten brief minutes have felt like hours. It's as if time has gotten soft. A minute feels stretched, like a big wad of saltwater taffy being pulled before it's cut.

I motion to get up, but Nicholas insists on a few more minutes. I have lists to make, phone calls to return, stories to write, meals to prepare, mail to open, bills to pay. The Sunday paper still lies in an unread heap on the dusty piano. My thoughts begin to scramble again, and I have the urge to fall to the floor and start gathering them with my bare hands. I stay put.

I study my son's face, thinking I will remember every detail forever, but the weeks pass, and he is changing again. He is a variation on a theme. We try to capture his essence in photographs, but something always gets lost in the translation. It's as if we're trying to take a four-by-six picture of the Grand Canyon.

I hold him, and I feel it again: blessed and bound. But this is different than two years ago.

We sway back and forth, Nicholas is fitted to me like a puzzle piece. I feel the irrepressible glory of the moment. The luxury. The privilege. The ache. It is all so temporary.

He is passing through. Soon, he'll be out chasing a firefly. Chasing a dream. A girl at school. And this rocker will be still.

How long can this possibly last—the two of us rocking without words? How strange it is to be so acutely aware of a moment that will merely slip into the sleepy unconscious, never to be recalled or retrieved. The two of us rock for the moment, in the moment, an image fated to fade.

This twosome shall pass.

When he asks me to "rock a lidda bit mo," I think, Who am I to put limits on bonding, to deny him an extra eight minutes as opposed to two? He's asking me for more *time,* not a remote-controlled fire truck. This is the first real sign to me that he is beginning to understand the unspoken dynamics of relationship. I realize that it is the adult who creates the threshold for connection, who imposes restraints on intimacy, telling a child, "That's enough now," when it isn't. *We* interrupt the moment and curb our togetherness under the guise of setting limits, instead of allowing ourselves to feel the full impact of this bond—the effects of it, the threat, the rewards.

I remember playing street games on our block when I was a little girl. Dozens of us would chase each other, a ball, or a bucket, until we were tired and sweaty and my parents flicked the porch light on and off like air traffic control to signal us in for the night. Even back then, before any of us had completely lost our baby teeth, surrender was something the losing team did because they weren't good enough, strong enough, brave enough. Growing up, most of the people I knew thought surrender was an act of weakness. We all learned that on the playground, in the classroom, on the track, in love. Surrender equaled loss.

I come to the rocker with this story, bringing all these images and notions to the chair, and one by one they come forth for review. Surrender as defeat. Surrender as weakness.

I have rocked with defense. I have rocked in fear of being depleted, with the threat of my baby's needs looming over my head like a thundercloud—the needs that we, as parents, are so anxious will overtake us and do us in. I rocked with a head full of dueling notions, feeling both needed and ineffective, nurturing and incapable of consolation, paradoxically fearful and hopeful of losing myself.

How could I love this child honestly, unconditionally, if a part of me is afraid of him, of myself—of us? How could I really see who he is and nurture who he is meant to be, with a sheath of doubt shrouding my perceptions of him? And might that not alter his authentic self, the original path he was meant to pave in this life?

I lift the veil. Now I can see that behind it, I felt the dread of being consumed, of losing myself forever, of slowing down long enough to know the deep crevices within me filled with dust and cowardice, the places where my spirit had begun to calcify and turn brittle.

I recognize the churning of my own unfulfilled needs, the agony of my longings. It is little wonder that we hold our heart's desire at arm's length for fear of having and losing those we love. Surrendering to my baby, I finally realize, is not at all about defeat or loss or weakness. It's not about letting the baby drive me up the wall or off the road. It is about seeing with the heart.

I must see him as I see myself, see his needs as I would have someone see mine, allowing him the same right to be human—to be himself. Surrender is about being open, letting in and offering a depth of love and vulnerability and commitment—in motherhood and in marriage—that I might have previously yearned for at a distance.

In a sense, it is about giving up, giving up the barrier between love and fear. In doing so, I feel more connected—to myself, my son, my husband, God, the history of time. Somehow, sitting here, I feel related to every mother who ever rocked a baby in her arms.

I surrender.

I had imagined, as every pregnant woman does, that loving my baby would be a simple act of bonding. In this rocker, two years later, I am stunned by the power and the complexity of that act. There is nothing simple about fear, and nothing simple about loving with it. To truly surrender, I realize, is to let go of fear—to surrender it.

My son and I have been getting to know each other. We weather our storms of insecurity, our fears of falling, of failing, of loss. Once, we were lost on the open sea, with no sign of the shore, and we nestled together and rocked and rocked and rocked our way home.

CHAPTER TWENTY-ONE

The Closet

here is a little space in the kitchen of my childhood where the open door meets the wall. A perfect equilateral triangle. My favorite hiding place.

"Ready, here comes you!" calls out Nicholas.

I stand in the corner, the triangle behind the open door in his room, sucking in my gut. He tiptoes toward me and pokes his nose in the crack.

"Mommy, you found you!" he trumpets.

Dave, Nicholas, and I are on our way home one balmy, overcast afternoon. We drive leisurely through the neighborhood, browsing, gazing at houses with wraparound porches and sprawling backyards.

Nicholas refers to our four-by-six-foot balcony as his backyard. Our two-bedroom apartment is the only home he has known. This is where we live right now. He does not feel cramped. He doesn't want a bigger playroom, or fantasize about a fenced-in yard away from the street.

But Dave and I are not quite as easy to please. We move the

couch under the window, heave the piano over to the fireplace, haul the dining-room table up from the basement. Six months later, we roll the piano to the window, and push the couch against the fireplace, which no doubt violates the feng shui tenet about never blocking fire.

But the fire is in my belly. How can I make this house a home?

I have grated two cups of mozzarella; diced onion, carrots, celery, zucchini, and minced garlic; and browned a pound of ground beef. The spaghetti sauce is bubbling. Diana Krall is crooning "Popsicle Toes" out of two small speakers on the living-room floor. The light of an approaching evening is casting shadows on the walls.

Dave and Nicholas are nowhere in sight. It has been about an hour since I last saw them reading books in the basement. I turn the element down to let the sauce simmer, dry my hands, and wander through the house. On my way downstairs, I hear the creak of wooden boards under my socks. The basement is silent. Two caps are off their markers. A drawing of a fire engine in green lines still smells of ink. Books are strewn all over the chair and floor. I walk through the hallway upstairs and begin to hear faint, muffled voices, which I follow to our dusky bedroom.

A light flickers on and off behind the door of our walk-in closet, like a giant firefly searching for the exit. As I reach for the knob, I hear a roomful of people narrating a story, each with a different pitch and accent, and a tiny spirited voice of conviction peppering the plot with intrigue and laughter. I knock three times gently. The closet is quiet.

"Who's der?" calls Nicholas.

"Who eez eet?" asks Topo Gigio in falsetto, the voice of one of the ninety-two characters that have come to live inside Dave's head since he became a father.

I slowly turn the knob and pull it toward me. There, in the

dark, is my husband sporting ski goggles and holding an *I Spy* book, and our son pointing a flashlight at me.

"Hi, Mommy!" he chirps. "We read books in da closet!"

I flick on the light switch. They both squint. Here, beneath a curtain of suit jackets, slacks, and shoes, Dave and Nicholas are surrounded by books, pillows, teddy bears, and dogs, a child's wooden banjo, a pair of green binoculars, a kaleidoscope, a small drum and metal whisk, three different kinds of hats, a purple snorkel, black Mickey Mouse glasses, a rubber snake, a cow puppet, and two orange pom-poms. Did I forget something? Oh yes, a plate of cookie crumbs and two empty glasses.

The racks of clothes hanging above and around them in a U look like spectators in the world's smallest amphitheater.

"This looks like fun," I say.

"Snow, snow, snow," Dave recites in his Dr. Seuss voice. "Let's go, go, go!"

"Go, go, go!" echoes Nicholas, wearing his winter hat. He is cramped in this dinky walk-in, with barely enough room to wave his arms, but he could not be more comfortable if he were lying buck naked on a cloud.

I realize, standing in the doorway, that Dave has created more of a home inside this closet than there is in the walls that surround it.

As I look at the big goofball with goggles and at the toddler who reveres him, I remember the first time Dave and I met, in college. I was going to play the piano and sing an Elton John tune in a school variety show, and he was preparing to spoof a newscast with pop songs to punctuate his headlines. Hair parted and greased to each side, he was wearing an oversized sports jacket, thick black eyeglasses with masking tape over the bridge, and a makeshift moustache.

"What's that?" I asked, pointing to the dead caterpillar on his upper lip.

"Tea leaves and Vaseline," he answered.

Years after that pithy backstage exchange, he sits on a closet floor, singing Clarisse's song from *Rudolph the Red-Nosed Reindeer*.

There's always tomorrow for dreams to come true.

I shake my head and snicker. He espies me through orange lenses.

"She tinks I'm cute! She tinks I'm cu-ute!"

What makes a home? The bricks and mortar? Or the people who inhabit it? I think about pacts and promises we make at the altar, at conception, in the delivery room, at the frontier of parenthood, the vows we all make to ourselves to do our best, and to each other to respect each other's way—even if it contradicts our own. I think about how our pledges, these oaths of alliance and allegiance, get tested. How our beliefs get challenged by changing circumstances, nagging self-doubt, and the universal wish to be validated.

I really couldn't have known, in the years that preceded this moment, that the person wearing tea leaves on his upper lip would become so devoted a father. I could only have guessed that the diligent architecture student who regularly fell asleep on his drafting table at 3 a.m. would someday read to our son in the closet and spin magnificent tales.

I gaze at Nicholas and his dad, and wonder what our son will remember. Will he even vaguely recall these closet book readings? Or the scent of the carpet? Or Dave's sea-blue eyes as he painted word pictures in the air?

Standing in the doorway watching them, I think of my own father. My childhood memories of him are not borne of events, but of his essence. He used to wear this cologne that smelled like traveling. It reminded me of the river Seine and of ferry rides and of just-baked bread sold from a bakery window facing some cobbled street in Strasbourg. A whiff of it in the front vestibule of our old house and I remember his arrival home after business trips, with his bulging briefcases that were anything but brief. He smelled like jet lag. Trench-coaty and new. Before he could take his jacket and scarf off, my brother, sister, and I would wrap around him like vines, yearning to take the place of his coat sleeves, as leaves blew in the front door. With the changing seasons, my father's cologne smelled like patience. The park bench heard a lot of our conversations over the years. The maples too. They never judged, and rarely did he. Dad has always smelled like the passage of time. Constant. Stalwart. Eternal. Archival. A present moment so ultimately memorable, it's already alive in retrospect. Even now that I have a child of my own, my father still smells like home.

Nicholas's eyes are fixed on his own father, who is now wearing a construction hat in the closet and making bulldozing sounds, and I know, in the farthest reaches of our son's memory, these images will never make it past next year. Yet, somehow, I can sense them etching a lithograph of love and trust and security within him.

I could not have known that Dave would be such an emotionally accessible father, just as I could not have known what it would feel like to have somebody call me Mom every day for the rest of my life.

We can never know until we butt heads over whose way is better, whose way is right, until we feel the sting of criticism and the unforgiving armor of our defenses, until we come of age, that there is no "wrong" way when two people love a child well.

Pregnant with our first baby, I assumed that my husband and I would parent equally. I had no idea that we would not only be different parents, but that there could be valuable assets in those differences.

I don't do closet book readings with our son. It would seem odd to even suggest it to him. That's something Dave and Nicholas have created. Dave doesn't build pillow drum sets from the living-room sofa. That's something Nicholas and I call ours.

"Ladeez an' gennelmin, now fer yer lissining pleasure, Mommy plays boogie-woogie on da piano!" the two-and-a-half-year-old announcer bellows into his gourd microphone, as he accompanies me on his couch drums.

Dave acts out *The Great Knitting Needle Hunt* (by Paul Geraghty), hiding a knitting needle (a wooden chopstick) somewhere in the house and giving Nicholas clues in riddles to help him find it. He bakes bread with him as Uncle Louie, the ultracool, jazz-scatting horn player from one of Nicholas's favorite books, *Music over Manhattan*. And being the architect in the family, he builds three-dimensional helicopters and twin engine planes (with moving propellers, of course) out of TinkerToys.

Nicholas and I have a different repertoire of activities and our own way of relating to each other. We visit the local fire station a mile down the street, where he wants to stand between two shiny pumper trucks and serenade them.

In bumper-to-bumper traffic, we break into song:

"It's up to—" I croon.

"You!" he belts.

"New—"

"Yoke!"

"New—"

"Yoke!"

We go on scavenger hunts, make musical instruments out of paper towel rolls and foil, and make chocolate chip cookies while Nicholas talks to the ingredients. "Flour! Yer so soft! Do you wanna taste some butter?"

The days where I knew Nicholas more intimately than Dave (or thought I did) are long gone. As are the days when Nicholas would snub his father, choosing Mommy over Daddy for soothing, entertainment, and attention. Overnight, he has become Dave's groupie.

———

Nobody can force a bond to develop in a certain way or at a specific time between two people, regardless of their age and blood relation. Just as we bonded differently with our son, so has he with us. I could not expect him to have the same relationship with each parent if we are two unique people. Our relationships with him are not interchangeable.

We are like the space behind the door. An equilateral triangle. Equal sides, love, leading from different places to the apex, our boy.

Home is not a house, a tepee, an igloo, a mansion. It is something we build within us, behind our eyes, between our hearts. And maybe we can only truly understand its meaning when we are compelled to redefine it. This old home with a new addition.

CHAPTER TWENTY-TWO

Homeward Bound

finally feel good in my skin. At long last, after more than two and a half years of feeling distended by onerous, internal questions about my competency and my son's inner peace, my maternal instincts and I have become good friends. Eight hours of uninterrupted sleep at night have done wonders.

Nicholas, approaching three, is no longer an enigma to me. My boy and I have developed a kind of shorthand.

"Mommy, what are you doing?"

"I'm trying to decide what to wear," I say, standing in the closet.

"I know! Tupper-wear!"

Pa-dum-pum.

I feel healthy and happy, with enough time, hallelujah, to go to the end of a thought and let it run down like honey from a spoon in midair. I have achieved balance.

Mama got her groove back. Oh yeah, baby. Which is why it occurs to me that this would be a swell time to get pregnant.

I feel green as seaweed. I am horizontal, motionless, numb with nausea, lying on the edge of my bed in anticipation of how the slightest vibration—footstep, barely audible whisper, telephone ring—tickles the back of my throat like a feather.

"Mommy? How's yer baby growing ta-day?" Nicholas asks while I moan softly.

"Mommy'th . . . not . . . feelin . . . well . . . buh . . . I'll . . . feel . . . better . . . thoon . . . thweetie," I manage to utter.

He dashes down the hall and returns with a harmonica.

"I know what you need to feel better, Mommy," he exclaims. Then, he begins to breathe in and out of the harmonica with gusto, doing a little do-si-do at the foot of the bed.

"Mommy, you feel better now," he states emphatically, wiping the saliva from his chin.

Twenty weeks. We are hypnotized by a gray and white silhouette. A tiny arrow points out the ventricles, the vertebrae . . .

"Hi baby brother! It's me, yer big brother!" yells Nicholas, hurtling himself toward the screen.

"I'm gonna teach you how ta dance ta jazz music!"

Dave and I cry with sweet laughter. I feel warm tears trickle back into my ears as I lie there on the table in the dimly lit room with my son, whom I know so well, and this beating heart on a screen that belongs to my other son, whose face I couldn't pick out in a crowd.

On the fourth day of February, after laboring to my friend John Herberman's CD "Rhythms of the Sea" five consecutive times, my contractions coming in and out like the tide, Benjamin is born into a brilliant ray of sunshine at 1:12 p.m. Six pounds nine ounces of a brand-new human whose nose is still squished to the right from his cramped quarters, a one-minute-old boy who knows how to suckle already, a delicate being whose lids are the color of ripe watermelon and whose lovely lips look as if they are about to recite the love sonnets of Rainer Maria Rilke by heart.

I am a mother again.

I am in love again, something I secretly worried was an impossibility. Love someone *other* than Nicholas? Is this viable? Is it *necessary*?

Three hours after Ben has made his debut, I can hear Nicholas prancing down the hospital corridor, greeting the entire nurse's station.

"Hi, I'm Nicholas! I'm two. My birthday is in two weeks. I'm gonna meet my baby brother now. Bye."

I am sitting on the bed in my trendy light blue hospital gown, my hair in two braids. Baby Ben is asleep in the bassinet in front of me. My heart is pounding as Nicholas approaches our room with Dave. As they turn the corner, my firstborn son looks familiar and yet vaguely foreign, as if the chemical composition of our bond has been slightly rearranged in the last ten hours while he was busy making Play-Doh sandwiches at home with my mom and I was busy having another child whom I will also call my son for the rest of time.

Nicholas greets me like I am his long-lost love at the twenty-five-year high-school reunion. As I hold him and we sway back and forth for a few wonderful moments, I am strangely aware that there is someone else in the room.

"Sweetheart," I whisper into his curly hair, "Daddy and I have someone for you to meet."

Nicholas peers into the bassinet. He gasps and whispers, "My baby brother is here. Shhh! He's sleeping . . . Let's go to Ben and Jerry's!"

Bringing baby Ben home feels like a dream. Big brother holds him in his lap, and the road ahead looks uncluttered with the barbed wire of sibling jealousy. Phew. This is a breeze.

I pushed for three minutes. The baby's latch is perfect. Dave and I have been here before. I feel no anxiety. No breastfeeding pain. No doubts about how to soothe my newborn. No worries. Or as they say in Swahili, "Hakuna matata." (*There is no difficulty.*) Nicholas has made a stellar transition. Ben, a breathtaking beauty with the longest lashes I've ever seen, looks like a sleeper and doesn't seem to mind transportation, diapers, clothes, slings, pouches, water, strollers, phone calls after dark. I believe we have hit the jackpot. Break out the bubbly. Our family is complete.

Screeeech. Fade to black. Cut to me nursing the baby at 12:05 a.m., 2:34 a.m., 4:15 a.m., 6:02 a.m. Cut to Dave curled up next to Nicholas at 3:30 a.m. after the poor child dreams that there are furry black spiders in his bed or that his marching drum is in the oven. Cut to my crippling dreams of losing Nicholas in a crowd, of him falling off a cliff, going down the drain, dreams of having to choose between my sons as the road splits and crumbles while I am running for safety and I can't physically take both of them with me.

Dissolve to me two days after coming home from the hospital. I am in our dimly lit bedroom, swabbing the baby's navel with a moist cottonball.

"Mommy?" Nicholas calls from down the hall.

"Yes, sweetie," I answer. "I'm in here."

He walks into the room, and looks at me snapping up Ben's onesie on the changing table.

"That's okay," he says. "Daddy? Daddy?"

"Honey, what is it? Nicholas?" I call out after him, while he disappears down the hall to ask for his father's help instead.

I lower my head and can't for the life of me resist the tidal wave of grief that crashes through my chest.

"What's wrong?" asks my mother, who walks in at that moment.

I can't speak.

"What?" she insists.

"It's Nicholas," I choke. "I feel like everything's *changed* . . ."

And with that, I weep a river. My mother reaches around my crumpled shoulders, and I cry like a baby in her arms.

They call it juggling. But this isn't a circus act where I am spinning a chair on my chin and tossing colored balls in the air.

Last week, every hour of every day, I was here at home, inside the living room, the kitchen, the basement, with a three-year-old—who wants to build a volcano, make a planetarium, do a puppet show with me behind the couch, be a dolphin in a giant sofa aquarium—and with a newborn who thus far doesn't like to sleep much longer than forty-five minutes at a stretch all day and night. It's too frosty to go to the park. Too far to go to the mall with a baby who wails hysterically in the car seat. Too tiring to go to a friend's house to play where you have to be polite and conversational and talk about your children's development and sit in perfectly coiffed houses where all the toys and clothes have been neatly put away.

An hour after breakfast, I feel like it's already midnight. I try to organize big brother with craft supplies at the dining-room table. During baby brother's nap, big brother decides that it is necessary to yell for me at the top of his lungs while I am momentarily in the bathroom. By midday, both children are screaming. Baby is gassy. I try to nurse him for comfort. Nicholas, feeling feverish, wants me to hold him. I hold Ben in my left arm and Nicholas in my right, both of them crying in different pitches, the little one's rhythm a quarter note followed by two eighth notes and the big one holding court with a long, unbroken G. Their first duet. I sing along, rocking, humming, whimpering, deep-breathing, praying.

As I help both find their peace, strangely, amid the chaos of noise and needs, I find mine. It's as if it's so difficult, it becomes easy. So loud, it becomes quiet. The inherent polarity of turmoil.

My mind shuffles through stats and images, memories of

Nicholas as a baby, and I lay my perceptions of my firstborn over the ones of my second, like tracing paper. It's difficult to avoid the lure of comparisons. He's my serious one; he's my free spirit. Or the third one's payback for my easy ride with the second. Or my fourth was my reward for the hard time with number one. Maybe it's not about comparing them in the strictest sense, but more that we are psychologically, physically, and spiritually transformed by the first in a way that we cannot be by anyone else. Such is our initiation into parenthood.

Through our experience with the first child—with his or her personality, eccentricities, inclinations, needs—we learn to define ourselves as mothers. When our second child is different from the first in every way, we are thrust into a redefinition of ourselves, of motherhood, of our perceptions and choices. I can never unlearn what my first taught me. And yet these hard-won lessons may find little application in the mothering of my second child. I will learn new things from Benjamin, realize different aspects of motherhood and of myself that I couldn't have known in my years before him. I realize, in a cold sweat that often accompanies starkly obvious revelations, that these are two separate people. I must mother them equally and absolutely individually.

We nuzzle here silently, three tiny dots on the slippery slope of a learning curve, clinging for dear life.

"La-la-la-LAAA!" yells Nicholas repeatedly in an aggravatingly loud rendition of Beethoven's Fifth. Thank you, Elmo.

"Nicholas, please!" I shout back from across the room, after which Ben begins to cry. Great, now *I* have scared the baby. Is there a lesson is this madness? Note to self: Don't shout across the room to son about not shouting across the room.

Nicholas is about to play a drum solo on Benjamin's head with wooden spoons. Again. I can't leave him in the same room with the baby. Not even for a second. Bouncy seat is called bouncy for a reason.

"Baby Ben's head is very, very delicate, Nicholas," I point out. Again.

No response.

"We play drums on drums not on heads," I lay down the decree. "Okay?"

Silence.

"What color is cow poop?" he asks suddenly, as if it were on his mind all day.

"Is he jealous?" friends and strangers ask.

He has never demanded that the baby be returned, never wanted to leave his brother behind when the family went to the supermarket, a friend's house, or out of state. He includes his brother in his own introduction.

"Hi, I'm Nicholas. I'm three years old. I'm a big-boy brother. My brother's name is Benjamin. But I like to call him Ben-Ben."

And when someone jokes that they would like to keep Ben, Nicholas argues, "No! He's our family! He has to stay with *us*."

But since baby came home, big brother has gotten louder. Much louder. He calls for me in that 911 kind of way. The noise gets into my joints like his newborn cry of three years ago. He raises his volume, and I lower mine. He screams for me when I am right in front of him. I become Marcel Marceau, nodding and gesturing that I am right here and he is right there and there is no need to yell.

Dave phones from the corner of Thirty-fourth and Madison at 7:15 p.m., and Nicholas is shrieking loudly in my left ear to hang up and read him the *Meet the Orchestra* book while I simultaneously nurse the baby who is yelping at my breast because he has a bubble and Nicholas wants him to go to his crib so that I can read to him alone and I snap at my three-year-old to stop yelling and he looks at me with wounded eyes and then I feel flushed with helplessness and remorse wondering if this was ever the life I imagined for myself back when I was creative and busy with projects and dreams and big ideas. But then Dave sounds like he's in a hurry and the phone cuts out, and my mother offers to get Nicholas to sleep while I take the baby into my dark bedroom. The phone rings again, and I talk to Dave while I pat the baby's back and hear Nicholas whine for me behind the wall in his room where my mom sings to him. A few minutes later, I hear nothing but the faint humming of a Greek lullaby. The door opens slowly, my mother tiptoes out into the hallway with a thumbs-up sign, and I feel hollow as old driftwood.

The house is quiet. No more vigilance, protests, distractions, explanations, negotiations, strategies, second-guesses, self-doubt, reminders of dangerous places. But I feel sullied and incomplete. Something's nagging me like an argument with a spouse or a misunderstanding at work. This is the first night I didn't get to say goodnight to Nicholas before he fell asleep. I feel like he and I got lost tonight. Like maybe he's still lost somewhere in his dreams and I can't find him and we have to wait ten long hours before reuniting tomorrow morning.

I feel like he used to love me. Like I am betraying him while I tend to the baby.

He comes to the changing table where I'm putting on Ben's diaper and parrots lines from *Blue's Clues*.

"Did you see the mystery builder?" he whispers, his eyes darting around the bedroom. I ask him if he wants to build something out of Lego, or empty egg cartons and toothpicks. And he darts around to my other side to give me my line.

"You hafta say, 'Did he have a tail?'"

He asks for chocolate cake at 9 a.m., and when I say no, he slumps his shoulders like a cartoon character and shuffles off in slow motion, sighing in that theatrical way that cartoon people do.

I feel heartbreakingly divided. My longtime friend Deborah, mother of two teenage sons, gently reassures me that, in time, love grows. Not that we don't love our children from the moment we meet, but rather that it's a journey to go from the divided heart, feeling split between two small people who want you wholly, to the expanded heart that has allowed time and maturity to mellow it. A process that cannot be rushed, only trusted.

I sense that Nicholas is feeling divided as well. He is shifting gears, trying, I assume, to decipher the new geometry. Triangle to square. Does he now feel like a round peg?

His language has changed since our family expanded. Now, his yes may mean no depending on whether it's past 4 p.m. Now, a shrug could mean yes if the thermostat is set at seventy two and he's had a morning snack of Granny Smith apple slices and orange cheddar cut into two-inch sticks.

"We're going to a new music class this morning, Nicholas," I say at breakfast.

"No, thanks. I don't want to go," he says quietly.

"It sounds really fun. Let's go and give it a try."

"I'm too busy," he blurts.

"I'd like you to participate," I urge gently.

"What's 'participate' mean?"

"It means to do it, to join in an activity."

"Oh, I participated yesterday," he reasons.

An hour later, the table is cleared, our clothes and shoes are on, and Nicholas is ushering me down the front steps to the music class he doesn't want to go to.

"C'mon, Mom, we don't want to be late," he insists.

No means yes, yes means maybe, maybe means absolutely not on Tuesdays unless I'm wearing my favorite chartreuse sweatshirt.

Five months into mothering two equally important children with equally vital and legitimate needs, I arrive at my parents' house in my hometown with mastitis, strep throat, a vial of antibiotics, four suitcases, two kids, two car seats, a heavy heart, and a ticket with no return date. Dave has two business trips to the Far East in the next few weeks, so the kids and I will stay with my parents until he returns.

While Ben stays home with my mother, Nicholas and I go strawberry-picking and then take a tractor ride at a farm. We sample ice cream from every parlor in town. We dance to bagpipe music at an outdoor concert by the lake, chase dozens of children running across the grass, pick dandelions and buttercups, laugh, sit in trees listening to the musicians playing inside a white wooden gazebo under a moody lavender sky.

I watch Nicholas play. His chestnut curls dance with every step. He smells of sun lotion, mowed grass, and sweaty cotton. I revel in his joy. When was I ever this carefree? I wonder. Will I ever be again?

As the last notes of a saxophone solo echo into the black night, we gather our blankets and baseball caps and make our way down the hill to the car to beat the crowd.

"Bye, Lara! Bye, Blaise!" Nicholas calls out to his friends as I twist open a water bottle for him. "See ya tomorrow! Have a good night! Don't let da bedbugs bite! Sleep tight!"

But the next day when we visit the neighborhood swimming pool, Nicholas spends his time in the wading pool frantically trying to amass the plastic boats, shovels, and pails and rescue them from their watery demise down the drain.

"Is Daddy coming back soon?" he bawls while I prepare his dinner.

"Daddy will be here in ten days, honey," I say, taking out the calendar and holding him in my arms. "You want to mark the days with a big marker?"

"Oh, I miss him!" he laments.

So do I. Since we became parents of two, the math is straightforward: there is one child for each of us. It feels like Dave and I are on separate sailboats waving colored flags at each other from across a river, some kind of spousal semaphore to bridge the divide.

I comfort my three-year-old. The baby cries. My milk begins to come down. I whimper once under my breath. These days, from the time both children wake up at 6:30 a.m., I wonder how I'm going to muster the energy, patience, courage to make it through each hour of the day. Somehow, you just do it. You lead. You follow. You . . . participate. You do it with a fever, with a sore throat, with a pounding headache that makes you want to keep your eyes closed all day. You sit in traffic eating animal crackers, and somehow you discover that you have more fuel than you ever thought possible. It comes to you from your children, through them, because of them. You laugh at the knock-knock jokes that have no punchline. You walk uphill pushing sixty combined pounds of progeny in a stroller and sit in a rock field drawing chalk flowers and stars on flat stones with the older child while the younger one sleeps. You sponge up the spilled juice, separate the colors from the whites, listen to your children's unspoken concerns, decode the language of their fears, create a safe haven, teach them how to cope—even as you learn how yourself.

"I know you want Daddy to be here right now," I console, hugging him close while nursing the baby. "He'll be home soon, sweetheart. Would you like to call him?"

"No-o-o-o!" he wails.

Over the next two days, he tells me he misses Dave during every waking hour, about five times an hour. By nightfall, he cries a crescendo of fatigue, and bedtime becomes a land of the broken-hearted.

He can't lie flat, can't open his eyes long enough to read, outwardly refuses my understanding or affection. He wants water.

"I'll get it. You stay here in your warm bed, and I'll be right back."

He shadows me downstairs to the kitchen.

"I miss him, Momm-y," he continues now in his tired cry that is more a dry, spoken whine than a wet, mewling wail.

I have no more energy. It's past nine. My knees begin to buckle. My eyelids twitch with fatigue. I pour him some water.

"I mi-i-iss Da-a-add-y," he moans.

My blood races. I breathe deeply, tidy up an already clean kitchen, dial up our home number to check for messages while he sips.

"I miss Da—"

My circuitry is overloaded.

"Stop!" I whisper brusquely. "I *heard* you. You miss Daddy. I know. He'll be back soon. It's time to go to sleep!"

No messages. I hang up.

"But I miss—"

"Stop it."

"I mi—"

"STOP!"

An hour later, he's finally asleep, the baby is down, and I shuffle toward the den to slow-dance with depression—not the blue devils that Virginia Woolf wrote about, but the circumstantial, emotional blues that require rest, helping hands, love, books in hammocks, good food, silence, long walks, and a few hours alone.

I call in for phone messages again. Has anyone called me in my absence? Does anyone feel my absence? Does anybody know I exist? *Do* I exist? Is there anybody home?

"You have one unplayed message," says the robot lady.

A message! I press one to play . . .

"Stop it . . . I mi— . . . STOP!"

What? It sounds like a crank call, an eerie message that someone leaves from a phone booth before asking for ransom.

As I hold the cold receiver to my ear, trapped butterflies flapping wildly in my stomach, I suddenly recognize my own voice. In some miracle of modern telecommunications, the phone had not completely hung up and the machine had recorded my conversation with my son earlier that evening. And not the whole dialogue either—just the part where I had no more patience for an overtired three-year-old who missed his daddy.

I get the message.

"Press seven to delete . . ."

Flashback. Two years ago. Nicholas and I are sitting on linoleum tiles with eight other two-year-olds and their mothers. I am seven-and-a-half-months pregnant, sitting in a circle at a morning class of music, storytelling, ball pits, and organized mayhem. Twenty minutes into the session, the door opens and a woman attempts to walk in with her six-month-old boy on her left hip, a diaper bag on her right shoulder, an empty baby's car seat in her right hand, and her three-year-old on the floor in the doorway, whom she is ushering into the room with her right foot.

"Get up, Brian," she says, restraining the volume of her voice. She rolls him a few feet. He is in the fetal position, wearing a grin and a black soccer shirt, himself a human soccer ball at the moment.

The cross-legged children in a circle do itsy-bitsy-spider pantomimes, while the teacher and mothers sing in unison.

Brian's mother Karen is still in the doorway.

"Mo-o-o-ve," she insists in an aggravated whisper. She rolls her eyes at me and lets out a nervous laugh. She is dressed in a black sweater and clean dark blue jeans, her straight black collarbone-length hair pulled into a shiny ponytail. Her face is clear, angular, undecorated, her eyes brown and troubled.

"How are you doing?" she murmurs, as she sits next to me on the floor.

"Great," I say. "Another nine and a half weeks to go."

"That's good," she says, "but just wait. In a couple of years, you'll be rolling your son into the room like I did."

She chuckles that kind of chuckle that bears no malice, just the weight of a thousand regrets.

"See how great the two of you are now? How sweet your son is, how much patience you have for him?" she adds.

She pulls her baby boy back into her lap, planting an adoring kiss on his cheek.

"You won't have that patience anymore," she informs me. "I feel bad for my son, because it's not his fault, really. I just have no energy. No time. This baby doesn't sleep at night, and my three-year-old wants more from me now than he did before. And he carries on and has crying fits over nothing, and you try to be understanding, but there's just so much I can do. You feel so guilty. You feel like such a bad mother."

I listen, and nod politely, and think she could use a little couch time—and I don't mean for a nap. I could never be this woman's friend, I think, while she paints her death-defying portrait of mothering two. Rolling her child in the room with her foot? The lady needs a parenting course.

Two years later, I wonder where Karen is and whether she'd like to be my new best friend.

My dear girlfriend Lori has known me since we were both fourteen. She and Mark have three children, a seven-year-old girl and two boys under the age of four who are eighteen months apart.

"Do you ever feel like the mother from hell?" I ask her one evening way past my bedtime.

"Ha! Are you kidding? Every day, I cry about whether I've handled something properly. My four-year-old goes to his room now on his own to have a time-out before I've even told him to! What do you do with *that*? I never feel like I'm as good, as loving, as effective as I'd like to be."

Then she says something that hits me in the chest like a bass note.

"There's an economy of grace. We learn to forgive ourselves, and as we admit our shortcomings to our children, they learn it's okay to have shortcomings. We can have this grace for one another. That's God's economy. If we're not right, not perfect, it turns into a lifelong quest to be the person we can be."

Her words are nostalgic and soothing. In an instant, we are teenage poets, scribbling pithy lyrics on our plastic pencil cases in indelible ink, reading books for nourishment, suffering the pain of misfit adolescence—longing for the comfort of conformity at the same time that we recoil from it.

"Every day, I feel like Nicholas and I are getting further from where we used to be," I explain. "And sometimes, I think it must be terribly hard and confusing for him that I have someone else to care about."

"Lu, there are things our children need to learn from us that we don't even think of teaching them," she says, ministering to me. "I mean, what does a child need to learn about sharing your time, about sharing each other? What does a child need to learn about patience, tolerance . . . grace?"

We are mothers now, in the middle of the journey of our life, as Dante wrote, and we have come to ourselves within a dark wood where the straight way is lost.

Here I am, wandering in the wood. I search for the way home, the way into my child's heart, and the way out of my own.

Years Three and Four

CHAPTER TWENTY-THREE

Going-Away Day

gray midday haze hangs over the lake and right behind my eyes, the kind that lingers for hours. I stand in my parents' kitchen staring at hot bubbling water, hypnotically stirring a pot full of spiral noodles, wishing I could slip away, if just for a few moments, to a place where I can remember who I was when I wasn't who I am. If only to retrieve my once intact mind and return with it firmly in place. The Scarecrow looking for Oz.

I've been thinking about how much lighter this life of mothering seems when your child still loves you unconditionally, still wants you to kiss it better, still sees you as his panacea, his safe refuge, an extension of himself. And how infinitely complex things become when your baby grows into a boy who has—who needs—his own terms and conditions, refuses the sanctuary of your embrace, and tests your love for him by pushing you as far away as he might have you go without having you leave at all.

The noodles are overdone. I walk to the den to let my three-year-old son know lunch is almost ready, but the place is eerily silent. In a second, my heart is pounding the reverberating thumps of a gong. I shuffle quickly across the dining room to the glass sliding door. It's ajar.

Nicholas is gone.

I tear across the backyard to the lake, running with open arms, screaming his name into the humid air, eking out some foreign, primitive noise, my throat dry and constricted, howling as my eyes search the surface of the lake for a taupe baseball cap with a blue rim, but I see nothing except murky water, seaweed, and a rusty orange buoy bobbing affirmatively. I shriek Nicholas's name again as I charge around the front of the house, frenzied, brushing the row of cedars with my shoulder, cursing in my heart, damning myself, him, motherhood, for leading us to this ugly, wretched, surreal moment of chaos and failure.

I hear my breath, heavy and labored. Branches snap fast and clean beneath my shoes. I bang my shin on a wheelbarrow halfway in my path, toppling it sideways without stopping or flinching. The manicured landscape seems dense and tangled as jungle vines.

I can't breathe. I am in delivery. He's in my arms. I'm nursing him. We are blowing out candles on his cake. He's one. We are laughing. I am holding him in the rocker. He's asleep in my arms. I can't believe this is happening. I'm going to be sick. He was just here, for God's sake, just here a moment ago. *I was paying attention.* The adrenaline shakes consume my body. I stop suddenly and scream my son's name to the sky with my eyes closed.

"I'm right here, Mommy," chirps a barefoot boy, wearing an olive green T-shirt and no underwear. He is on the driveway with an oval rock in each palm. His smile is naked innocence. I want to crumble to the asphalt. I consider hauling his bare ass into the house and permanently nailing shut all the doors and windows.

It's noon. Nicholas chomps on a turkey sandwich with mayo, no mustard, as though nothing ever happened, his leg swinging under the glass kitchen table, and I sit in a wicker-and-wrought-iron chair with my bruised shin, staring at remnants of this morning's breakfast on the jam-smeared table, counting crumbs and hours until dusk. One savage minute of mortal dread, godlessness, and contempt has drained me for the day.

I occasionally gaze at him, this child of mine who recently is not mine at all but his own person. When did he learn to unlock that sliding door? The door with the lock that sticks, that has to be jimmied just so while you push the handle to the left, then suddenly and decidedly to the right, in order for it to open? When did he begin to feel that he could venture outside, out in the world, without asking me, telling me? Without me?

A couple of weeks after our return home, my son sits in a mid-morning funk, brow knit, shoulders slumped, legs in a pretzel, his curly chestnut hair tangled from a fitful night's sleep. This morning, Nicholas is in his nest, on the couch surrounded by a mountain of pillows, wearing his favorite faded truck pajamas that are one size too small. I go to my bedroom to put on jeans and a shirt, and when I come back into the living room holding baby Ben facing outward, Nicholas bounds to the glass storm door to watch the garbage truck dump the bin contents into its open mouth. I stand behind Nicholas, Ben peering over his brother's brown curls and I over Ben's bald head, the three of us a living totem pole, when suddenly the baby wraps his little fingers around Nicholas's locks.

"AHHHHHHHHHHH!"

I pry the baby's fingers loose, brush the follicles from his sweaty palms, and try to assuage my hysterical three-year-old who has collapsed like a folding chair at my feet with his head in his hands.

"Mommy," he says suddenly, his eyes brooding and wet, "I don't like you anymore."

I can't imagine I've heard him correctly.

"What did you say, honey?"

"You're not my friend," he continues, eyes averted. "I don't want to see you."

He will not look at me, not even for a second to check if I might be looking at him. His words are barely audible, delivered without inflection like a judge reading a sentence.

"You don't want to see me?" I repeat, stunned by this inaugural dissing of me by my beloved child, who I have, until this moment, been happy to say has liked me very much.

"Anymore," he adds, for the record.

"Never?"

"Never."

He gets up from the couch as if in slow motion and walks calmly into his bedroom mumbling something about a mess; then he proceeds to trash his room with a terrific sense of purpose. He is not screaming while hauling every toy off his shelves, but just quietly and systematically creating his own brand of bedlam, narrating his own rendition of the *Mister Rogers' Neighborhood* theme song.

"It's *not* a beautiful day in de neighborhood, *not* a beautiful day in de neighborhood, would you *not* be mine, could you *not* be mine . . ."

I watch and listen carefully, trying to compute the data, to fit the jarring pieces of this unanticipated puzzle into some kind of sensible portrait of my boy, the boy I suddenly don't recognize, the boy who doesn't want to see me anymore.

What did I do?

My son stares at the wall.

"What are you feeling?" I ask.

"I'm feeling mad," he says, studying the carpet.

"About what?"

"About *you*," he blurts.

Then he winds up and thumps me on the arm with his open hand.

"I'm not gonna kiss it better!" he vows.

I stand before him, wordless, marooned, unable to move.

"I don't want a Mommy," he adds coolly. "I just need Daddy."

My face feels hot and swollen, as if I had walked head-on into a colony of angry bees. I feel a tightening in my chest, a stab of pain in my sternum that snatches my breath. I can't take my eyes off of him, feeling somehow that if I look long enough, the boy I know will reemerge. Is he lost? Can I find him? Is he gone? Must I mourn him? Are we, the us of the last three years, gone too? *What happened?*

I watch, decoding his body language, and imagine in his face the sight of him as a baby waving his arms at me when I played hide-and-seek behind my hands, his smile wide and bright as a crescent moon.

Now, I seek while he hides.

Just a few months ago, we were up the street looking for flat rocks and drawing chalk fossils when he asked, "Mommy, what's de soul all about?" Just like that. One moment, we are hunched over a sea of dusty pebbles, and the next, he is waxing existential.

"Well," I started tentatively. "Soul is about, uh, feeling things deeply, um, like home, happiness, music, uh, a beautiful sunset or a prayer—"

"Oh, it's about de heart," he said, getting right to the point, my lips still parted in midsentence.

And here we are half a year later, on the other side of the galaxy, zero gravity, rock fossils a distant mirage.

"Mommy, am I growing right now?" he asks. We are sitting on his bedroom floor surrounded by a quarry of Lego pieces while the baby naps.

"Yes, you are growing a little bit every day."

"Are you growing too?" he inquires, without taking his eyes off the cruise ship he is building.

"Well, I won't get any bigger," I say slowly, wondering if I might be venturing into boggy land. "But I will get older."

"Older?"

He stops, gets up, and looks out the window.

"Just like you. You will grow up one day and be a man, maybe get married and have children. And then I would be a grandma to your children," I continue, feeling vaguely like I have now given him far too much information.

A late afternoon headache sends me to my pillow for a short nap. Ten minutes later, Nicholas bounds into the dark room strumming his guitar.

At first, I pretend not to see his silhouette in the doorway. My mother-in-law, Joan, is with Ben in the living room while Nicholas makes every effort to wake me, finally pouring a box of blocks over his brother's head and announcing a spectacular mess that I just had to see to believe. I get up from my bed and stomp into the living room.

I am prepared to promptly direct him to clean up and sit alone in his room to ponder his actions and my consequences. But instead, a sudden calm washes over me. His attention-seeking behavior was so absurdly overt that it begs the deeper existential question: *huh?*

I decide to pursue his lead.

"Nicholas, can you tell me why you don't want me to take a nap?" I ask him scrutinizing his face. He looks like a teenager with perfect skin.

"I want to throw you away," he announces matter-of-factly.

"The garbage truck is gonna come and pick you up."

"You want to throw me away?" I echo.

"Yes, you go in de garbage, Mommy."

"Is the garbage truck coming tonight?"

"Right now. To take you far, far away."

"Hmmm. I'll miss you very much."

"I won't miss you."

"Am I going for a long time?"

"Forever and ever and ever."

"Am I going alone?"

"No, I'm coming with you."

"Oh, we are both going in the garbage truck together?"

"Yup."

"With the poopy diapers and banana peels and salmon skins and coffee grinds?"

"Yup."

"Can we take a bath afterward?"

"Nope."

"What about the crusher?" I ask.

He is seized with panic.

"Oh no!" he wails. "It will break us into pieces!"

In an instant, he is inconsolable.

"Mommy," he agonizes, *"can we be put back together?"*

His body is coiled in my lap, arms and legs spilling over, too long to be tucked in completely. I hold him tightly while baby brother Ben gnaws on a teething ring, watching intently.

The sun went down an hour ago. Nicholas is lying across his plaid comforter, one cheek buried in a chartreuse pillow. I slip into his room and kneel down beside him, resting my palm on his head. Silently, he extends his arm, bent at the wrist, hooks it around my neck, and scoops me down toward him like his toy excavator. We lie forehead to forehead, his eyes closed in his dusky room. I gaze past the wisps of his hair, at the dark blue and gray patches of evening sky, at the planet decals on his window, at the "planet dat rhymes wit penis," and I realize that there is so much of parenting that calls forth our egos. Does he like me? Does he love me less now than he did before? Am I the best mother he could wish for? Does he appreciate me? What is his anger, discontent, fear, pain saying about *me*? What did *I* do?

How can we take our children's behavior seriously without taking it so personally?

We lie here, two parallel lines in silence.

"I guess it's just a going-away day," he mumbles.

The storms of separation are upon us. Fears of loss and abandonment clang like church bells. In one instance, getting out of the bath becomes traumatic as he grieves the loss of water down the drain.

"It's not ever coming back!" he wails as I dry his body and his tears.

A simple bedtime lullaby about the moon turns night into mourning when he laments that the sun has gone to "outer space for good."

"I can't believe it!" he cries. "It's gone, and I forgot to say good-bye to it!"

Chalk drawings on the sidewalk? The rain will wash them away. Play-Doh? It will dry out.

I try futilely to retrieve the falling pieces of his puzzle scattered by the gale force winds of his unexplained anger. I am sobered by the realization that these are actually *his* pieces to gather, to scatter, to assemble whenever and however it makes sense for him.

"I'm mad!" he bellows.

"Why?" I ask.

"For a reason."

"What reason?"

"I don't know," he answers quietly, taken aback by his own confusion.

He wants me to move away closer. To go far, far away and not leave his side. He wants to shoo me like a black fly, and when I stand up to move, he implores me to stay. Lying next to him in the dark, I struggle with his inner war and my splintered ego and my heart urging me to listen, listen.

What is he really telling me?

Can we be put back together?

It can never be the "way" it was when Nicholas and I were a twosome with no other children to share my heart, my time, my attention. He must unwittingly sense that.

Can we be put back together? How does a mother convince a child that nothing is broken when he feels that kind of anguish? When he wants to repair every damaged object—a fractured toy, a torn page in a book a snapped twig—in order to restore it to its original form? Or break it in a fit of tears?

And if he didn't have the words? What might a child do to let his mother know he is anxious about losing his beloved place with her? Would he regress? Become clingier? Punitive? Smear his diaper contents on the walls? My friend's daughter became mother's little helper, while another friend's son climbed onto the stove or countertops every time his mother tended to his baby sister. How can we be sure that one child doesn't feel cast aside in favor of another?

The mayhem of change tests the integrity of our bonds, of our characters. The turbulence within my son tests my humanity, my compassion, my commitment. Can I let him hate me even as he loves me? Can I allow him to reject me, secure in the knowledge that I won't abandon him? Can I love him with due patience even as he leads me along these unlit, uncharted back roads I otherwise might have never chosen to travel?

As I lie beside him, I can feel his three-year-old heart breaking. I am humbled by my powerlessness, unable to explain this rite of passage to him, to remove it from his path. I remind him of his place in our hearts, in the world, of his safety, of our unconditional love, of his favorite things.

"Strawberries, sand between your toes, chocolate sprinkles on ice cream sundaes, big band music, sweet potato fries, construction vehicles, collecting acorns," I whisper slowly. His tears are dry and his limbs still.

"I love you forever," I whisper as I tenderly kiss and hug him goodnight.

"I don't love you forever," he whispers back.

He leaves a trail as the weeks pass. I follow his cues, using his compass to guide both of us.

"Mommy?" he asks earnestly one morning, still in his green dinosaur pajamas. "Who will be my mommy when you grow younger?"

"What do you mean?" both Dave and I ask in unison.

"When you get younger, will I have *another* mommy? Who will it be?" he wonders, his face filled with terrible concern.

I stand by the kitchen sink with wet hands, baffled, breathless. And then a fuse blows in the back of my mind. All that talk of growing up, of becoming older, of me becoming a grandma someday, has been churning in him. Could he have understood from that conversation that I would not always be his mother? And if he has been considering my eventual departure or loss—or replacement—on his small shoulders for even a minute, let alone days or weeks, what kind of unspeakable sorrow and terror and blind fury has he been harboring in his tiny beating heart?

His clues have led me to the place where I started. Here is a three-year-old, grappling with his own growth, feeling at once happy that he is a "big-boy brother" and equally unsure of where all of this will lead him—and us. He asks me if Ben will always be a baby. He wonders who he will be if he isn't who he is now. But if we are who we are right now, he calculates, how can we be different? How will things be if they aren't exactly as they are at this moment? Who will we be? Where will we be?

Be gone, Mommy. Go very far away.

Could he be casting me away before he loses me? Or checking to see if I might reject him under inclement conditions?

I suddenly understand his wrath with me for growing up, for his own growing up, for having another baby who will grow up too. I pull up a chair, and feel his pain so clearly now I could drown in my own tears right here at the dining-room table. We have been to the edge of the universe and back, and we haven't even finished breakfast.

The other day, I turned on the TV on my way to the kitchen and heard a group of women sharing their private, negative feelings about motherhood.

"But it's all worth it," one mother finally said in conclusion, "because of the unconditional love your children give you." Thunderous applause.

And I thought of garbage trucks. I stood there with a dirty diaper balled up in my hand, the baby in his playpen next to me and Nicholas lying on his bedroom carpet playing with a fleet of small fire engines, and I wondered how a mother can make sense of her experience and her emotions when unconditional love feels unilateral. What then? Is it all *not* worth it?

We nurture our children from conception, conscious of our efforts and their responses, unconscious of the ways in which our family scripts play out on their stage. What does this kind of love require from us? How daunting it is for parents to love a child with the awareness of our destined losses, to mine the depths of our souls in search of the courage to question our own motivations, our intentions, our authority. No other circumstance in our lives asks us to devote our sensibilities to the development of another person for the ultimate purpose of letting him or her go. The duty of letting go.

As we stand at the cusp of change, I am tempted to draw an outline around Nicholas's world, as if to gently lasso it—him—back into the fold. But I can't. The fold is in the process of becoming both his safe haven and the place to which he can return over time, if he chooses, after his journeys away from it. I must learn to let him leave the fold in small, intangible steps. To allow, even delight in, his unfolding.

"Mommy, why do they call it life?" he asks, lying on his arm and backing up a yellow dump truck across the basement carpet.

"I don't know," I say. "Good question."

"How do they make lights?"

"Well," I say, "lights are made with wires and a glass bulb."

"Oh, how do they milk a cow?" he adds.

"Cows have udders," I begin.

"Why do we have eyes?" he wonders.

"To see," I say.

"Why do we need to see?" he insists.

The questions come in rapid succession, his hungering curiosity asking for refills: Where is love? How do they make color? Why is there a conductor of an orchestra and a conductor of a train? Does ketchup stain if I'm wearing a red shirt? Why is there camouflage? Is God inside my body? Do we die forever? When we die, where do we die to? Do we leave the house?

"Are you gonna be a grama soon?" he asks, sitting up for the answer.

"Not for a very, very long time," I say.

"Don't be a grama, okay?"

"Okay."

"Don't grow older," he says, his tone innocent and resolute, his eyes moist with hope and fear.

I gulp, stemming a flood of emotion.

"Nicholas," I assure him, "I'll *always* be your mommy."

He pauses.

"Forever and ever?" he asks, his eyebrows forming a teepee.

"And ever. Amen," we say together.

"Yippeeeeee!" he squeals and clasps his arms around my neck.

"Mommy, I want to tell you something," he announces. He stands in front of my chair, his hands on my knees, as if he has good news to report.

"I don't want you to be gone anymore now," he smiles. His eyes meet mine emphatically.

"I'm glad," I say, "cause I really like it here."

"You're welcome," he replies and walks over to his train set in quick little steps, the kiloton weights off his ankles.

"I love you big as the sky, sweetheart."

"Tha-a-anks," he says liltingly from across the room.

"You're welcome, Nicholas. You're welcome."

CHAPTER TWENTY-FOUR

The Buck-Twenty-Five Stops Here

icholas is squatted at the base of the dining-room table rifling through our junk mail. His nimble little fingers flip through a toy catalog, when he suddenly slams his palms on a page.

"Mommy-y-y!" he screams. "Lo-o-ok it de-ez *dru-ums*!"

"Ooh! They look like the drum section you made over there," I note, pointing to the arc of mixing bowls on the living-room floor, the cookie rack leaning against the couch, and the metal spatula he has slipped in between the seat cushions as his hi-hat cymbal.

These days, our house is filled with makeshift instruments, popsicle-stick boomerangs, hard hats, books, blocks, talking toys, Lego, trucks, magnetic trains with unrelated parts attached to them like cabooses—paper clips, a tea strainer in the shape of a tiny house, and the little metal piece that fits inside the garlic press. In fact, whenever I need the garlic press, I know it's behind the couch—next to the mixing-bowl snare drum.

"Cin we get dem?" he asks without lifting his eyes from the page.

"It *is* a nice drum set, honey, but," I stall, "it costs a hundred dollars."

"Oh!" he bawls into my collarbone. "It's too many monies!"

He sniffs, wipes his nose on my shirt sleeve, and then says, "I guess we juss hafta get more monies."

"Hmm. From where?"

"De bank."

"Actually, *we* have to put money into the bank so that the bank can give it to us when we need it."

"Let's do it!"

"Well, money comes from working. Then we put that money in the bank and use it a little at a time to pay for food and electricity and our car and many other things. Whatever is leftover, we save."

About a month later, Nicholas and I are out for a stroll. He gathers small rocks and puts them in his left pants pocket.

". . . eighteen, nineteen, twenty!" he announces, as he places each pebble in my cupped palms, then returns each one to his pocket.

"That's quite a collection," I say, grinning at his lopsided pants.

"I'm saving dem."

"I see. For what?"

"To buy doze drums." He walks a few paces, his khakis weighed down by rock coins.

A few days later, on our way back from gym class, we stop in a local music shop where he is amazed to see the shiny instruments up close.

"Omigosh! A gold trombone! A silver trumpet! One an' a hundred cymbals!" he shrieks, dwarfed by ten thousand square feet of floor-to-ceiling musical merchandise. Rows of electric guitars in all the colors of the rainbow. A wall of glittering cymbals in various sizes. A room of bongos from eight inches to four feet tall. And an area designated for drums. He approaches tentatively, trying to absorb the landscape.

"Cin I play doze black ones?" he whispers.

The store manager, who has been shadowing us in an unobtrusive way, nods approvingly, helps my son up onto the black adult-sized stool, hands him a pair of wooden drumsticks, and steps back a few feet to watch. Without warning or fanfare, Nicholas launches into a fevered drum solo the likes of which I never imagined from his little hands. He plays his heart out for five minutes straight, not glancing up even once at me, the manager, or the crowd that has now gathered around in the aisle. The set is ridiculously big for him. His size-eleven sneakers are dangling three inches above the bass pedal. With every cymbal crash, he nearly falls off the stool. I watch with a sloppy grin and puddly eyes, not because he's got some modicum of musical talent, but because when he's expressing it he looks as if he has swallowed a warm breeze.

"We could have the set delivered to your house by tomorrow morning," quips the manager.

Before we leave, Nicholas scurries around the place chanting good-bye to the violins, clarinets, and xylophones, and he waves to the upright bass. On the drive home, I feel a strange mix of pride, joy, and guilt. By taking him to the music store, letting him play, and then leaving the drums behind, was I pleasing him—or teasing him?

"Do you think we ought to get him a set?" I ask my husband that night.

"How much is it?"

"Two hundred and forty-nine dollars," I wince.

We don't splurge easily, especially when it's something for a person less than forty inches tall whose interests are subject to sweeping changes during the course of an hour.

"The red drum set in the catalog is a hundred dollars, and there's also a blue one for thirty-nine ninety-five," I say, laying out our options. "Maybe we could order the forty-dollar set and see where he is with this in six months."

Too many monies. Did I really want Nicholas to think the only reason we wouldn't buy the drum set was the hefty price tag? I don't want him to think this is an issue of acquisition versus deprivation. What if we had the money to buy the drums and anything else his little heart happened to desire? Would we? What if the drums were free, if we had, say, won a toy lottery and a truckload of merchandise was scheduled to be delivered every year for the next ten years? Would we accept, split the booty with the rest of the neighborhood, or donate the whole cargo outright?

I know a boy whose mother buys him two of everything. Two bikes, two remote-controlled monster trucks, two DVDs of the same movie, two pairs of skis.

"In case one gets lost or broken," he reasons.

This reminds me of a classic moment I witnessed in Manhattan at the corner of Sixty-eighth and Columbus, before I was ever pregnant. A teenage boy was dribbling a basketball on the sidewalk, inches from the curb. His mother, standing next to him, said, "If that goes in the street, I'm not buying you another one."

"That's okay," he retorted, "I have two more at home."

Nicholas's three-year-old pal Jack owns three remote-controlled jumbo fire engines with foot-long ladders and sirens that can be heard from a block away. Justin has two bulldozers the size of cocker spaniels and a racing car fast enough to get pulled over for a moving violation. Shari has a dollhouse big enough to sleep in. Mark has enough Legos to build a lovely deck off the kitchen.

Nicholas has his share of toys too. But somehow, so far, most of his favorite playthings are household objects: the colander he wears as an astronaut helmet, the metal sieve he turns into a magnifying glass for his bug expeditions, the rolling carry-on suitcase he uses as an indoor lawn mower, the rhythm section he assembles using two whisks and throw pillows from the couch. Yet there's something about a makeshift toy that compels a parent to want to replace it with the real thing.

The cardboard box sits on our black rubber porch mat like a houseguest who wasn't invited. I look at it with forced detachment. *One false move and it's back to the factory for you, Boom-Boom.* I feel irrationally protective. What will become of that couch drum set, the mixing bowl snare, and the hi-hat spatula?

That night, while Nicholas is asleep, Dave and I carry the box down the basement steps to the middle of the room, open it, and begin assembly.

"This looks a lot smaller than in the catalog," we mumble in unison.

"Do you think he'll mind?" I ask.

"Do you think he'll notice?"

We sit back and stare at the flimsy blue drum set that took us a whole thirty-five seconds to put together.

"I don't know," I hesitate. "I hope he likes it."

In the morning, while Dave and Nicholas are making pancakes and Ben is sleeping, I take the new set into Nicholas's bedroom. Recently, he has made a game of playing music store. He's the store manager, and Dave and I are customers. He invites us in for a demonstration of his instruments: his pan flute that he made out of Tinkertoys, his guitar that we made together from a shoebox and rubber bands, his toy trumpet and sax, Dave's harmonica, and his plastic battery-operated piano that plays the extended-mix version of "Jingle Bells" on speed.

This morning, we reverse roles.

"C'mon in," I call out from inside his room. A three-and-a-half-year-old boy in green dump-truck pajamas walks in slowly, takes one look at the drum set, gasps, and freezes.

"Thank you, thank you, *thank you!*" he gushes, his hazel eyes glistening.

Dave and I are rather happy with ourselves. Awestruck, our son sits down on the wobbly black stool, picks up two brown drumsticks, gazing at them as if they were magic wands. He begins to play. The set falls over twice. His stool tips. The cymbal topples off the stand, and he replaces it several times. Dave and I glance at each other. Both of us are wearing our Cheap-pile-of-crap-we-should-have-bought-the-other-set face. Nicholas, on the other hand, is still smiling.

But something interesting begins to unfold. Ten minutes after his solo in the bedroom mirror, he gathers his ice bucket, metal mixing bowl, and empty oatmeal carton around his new set. Over the next few weeks, the new blue set with the stars on the bass drum sits in his room, a thin blanket of dust coating the silver cymbal, until one afternoon when Nicholas is inspired to experiment with various drumsticks. A wooden spoon. A turkey baster.

"Oh-h-h, no-o-o!" he cries down the hall. I bolt to his room and find him sitting in his bass drum, heels pointing to the ceiling.

"It broke," he says, with a look of shock, disappointment, and intrigue. He tips himself sideways, crawls out from the plastic shards, and stares at what's left of his drum set. Soon, he crouches down on his hands and knees, places the remaining snare, cymbal, and tom-tom on the floor in a cluster, picks up his sticks, and begins to play his broken drums with giddy pleasure. Eventually, he is back to his original percussion ensemble made from kitchen utensils, mixing bowls, and an empty oatmeal carton along with the remnants of his new broken drum set.

So, there you have it. Dave and I blew fifty-three bucks. What can I say?

"You know how many things my husband and I have bought for our kids over the last two years that sit in the closet or that we gave away?" asks my friend Diane. "Bags and bags of stuff, hundreds, no, thousands of dollars down the drain, in the attic, or worse, in the dumpster."

I guess the spending thing is only one part of my queasiness. I mean, would I love to go back and save every penny that we spent needlessly in our lives, before and after children? You bet your silver dollar.

I think what's really nagging me is that I'm not sure what buying more and more toys for a child does to his imagination. Would he still have the urge to invent a forklift out of chopsticks and adhesive tape attached to the front of another vehicle? If I regularly replace his inspiration with merchandise, something tells me he might become disconnected from his own ideas. And what then? Wouldn't a person then gradually yearn for *things* to fill the void? How would he see himself in the world from his vantage point of easy acquisition?

I once read that a fulfilled need is a building block of self-esteem. But a fulfilled *want*? I don't know. Is there any way to cut envy, boredom, and indifference off at the pass? How early can a person begin to feel the first pangs of general dissatisfaction, an inner restlessness that there is never enough?

I realize now that just because a child really really really wants a new toy doesn't necessarily mean he or she really really really *wants* it. When I buy my three-and-a-half-year-old bigger, better trucks, I invariably watch him get frustrated; they break easily or don't do what he expects them to do. Then I notice that he reuses the parts to make a new toy, a truck that he likes more than the one he saw on the store shelf. He even renames it.

We talk a blue streak to our kids about the price of things, about what's expensive and what's on sale. They know the value of many things. But do they know our *values*? How early can a person begin to have a set of values and live by them?

Parents are so often warned about spoiling babies with too much love and attention, cautioned against picking them up when they cry to provide comfort. People try to convince us that we ought to place limits on babies to prevent spoiling later on, but by the time "later on" is here, we may be planting the seeds of a confusing value system, rewarding "good" behavior with goods—material incentives to be kind, cooperative, honest, trustworthy. As parents, do we want our children to grow up and believe the world is their oyster—or that they can buy that oyster, compete for it, maybe even take it from someone else who has earned it?

There are lessons in the catalog caper.

My son wants to have more in part because there's more to have. At three and a half, he is old enough to plead for a Ride-on Excavator, to offer his toys for donation in exchange for it. He's too young to realize that he will play with it for four days, then use it as a climbing apparatus until it breaks. Too young to know that by the age of twenty, the average child will have received thirty-three thousand dollars in toys and allowance.

Obviously, we will always buy things for our children. But how does our gift-giving affect our children's behavior?

Nicholas's buddy Billy has an endless supply of toys. Under his bed, unopened boxes of brand-new train sets, games, and books lie in the dark among the dustballs. Yet, at four, he has already lost interest in what he owns. His focus is on the *next* toy. So he has no qualms about letting his pal Nicholas borrow whatever he wants. Not because Billy's feeling particularly generous, but because he is sharing by apathy. It's as if he looks around his overstocked play area and sees an empty room. On the other hand, I've noticed that

Nicholas seems less inclined to share his trucks for fear that some-one "might break something."

I wonder if there isn't a time for giving and a time for holding off until a child may be more receptive to the gift, more able to cope with it. Take Christmas morning. Like any child, Nicholas's excitement is palpable. While he plays with his new toy recycling truck, we offer him another present. Now, he's playing his new little bongo. By the third gift, he becomes giddy, distracted. By the fifth, overwhelmed. By the end, sapped. He doesn't know *what* to play with anymore. If you were to ask him what he got for Christmas, I bet he would draw a temporary blank, eventually name one thing, then spend the rest of the afternoon playing with his favorite "toy"—the curly ribbon from the box.

"Look, Mommy! It's a new kinda yo-yo called a Boingy-Boing!"

When the tree is dismantled a few weeks later, Dave and I are busy wrapping up decorations and lights, while Nicholas sits at the top of the basement stairs entranced by an ornamental string of gold and silver beads that he releases from his hands inch by inch, watching intently as it tumbles down the stairs to the plat-form below.

"What are you doing, kiddo?" we beckon from across the room.

"I'm making a waterfall," he whispers.

Few parents can imagine Christmas morning or a child's birth-day party *without* the onslaught of presents. My girlfriend Nina, mother of twins, lives in a house with a backyard the size of a mu-nicipal park. Her driveway winds through a small forest then re-veals a breathtaking landscape that is, well, her lawn. Nina's son and daughter grow strawberries, plant tulip bulbs, feed the fish and tur-tles in their pond, and have a grand old time learning about mulch, responsibility, love, and the mysteries of the food chain. For her children's third birthday, Nina sent out twenty cards from the twins with this request:

Your gift to us is to join us
in celebrating our third birthday!
If you would like to bring a present,
we would love to donate it on your behalf.

The party was a smash. Cake was great. Mickey and Minnie dropped in for a photo op. The next day, Nina and her kids drove a carload of gifts over to a family shelter where her three-year-olds parted with two dozen wrapped boxes without batting an eye.

Nicholas and I have begun our latest tango in which he begs sweetly for a toy vehicle too remarkable to pass up and I graciously decline.

"Juss dis one and no more," he bargains.

"We're not going to buy that truck today."

"Juss dis one, and dat's it," he persists.

"Not today, honey."

One afternoon, I return from the city with a red fire engine that fits perfectly in the palm of my hand.

"Oh, Mommy-y-y! I love it! I love it!" he squeals. He stares at it with rapture; then he cocks his head and wonders with a beguiling smile, "Why did you get dis for me?"

I am suddenly at a loss for words. Why *did* I get it? What am I telling him?

What are a parent's motivations? Do we buy to placate? To win affection? To console or reward? To apologize? To buy obedience, compliance, cooperation? To compete or keep up with other parents? To prove our love? Our worth? To relieve a child's boredom—on our own? To fulfill our own unresolved needs? Or maybe to compensate for our lack of time and attention?

Granted, there are those times when you just want to make your kid happy.

But sometimes, there's the price of a gift, and then there's the cost of buying it.

Standing in a store aisle, a couple argues over whether or not to get a children's table-and-chair set.

"Where are we gonna put it?" the husband groans.

"In the living room, near the couch," the wife insists.

"It's two hundred dollars. Do we really need this thing?"

Their three-year-old daughter, leaning on the handle of an oversized grocery cart, listens intently to her parents debate the pros and cons of buying her a present. Dad shakes his head, huffs, and heaves the big box into an empty cart.

"Merry Christmas, sweetie. This is your gift, okay?" says the mother to her child. And by the look on the little girl's face, it looks as if she's saying, Uh, no thanks, you can keep it.

Nicholas may want the drums, the digger, the didgeridoo. But he's still young enough to dream, to feel the thrill of his own imagination.

How does a parent preserve *that* reward? How do I let the baby drive *and* say no to the remote-controlled, jumbo log loader with side stabilizers?

Over the next couple of months, Nicholas continues to find rhythms in unlikely places. Brushing his teeth. Car horns. Popcorn popping in the microwave. There is no mention of a drum set or a catalog. I wonder if he has realized something about the value of his own inspiration.

At this point in his life, I can tell him that horsie-on-a-stick has to stay at the toy store with his family, and he puts the plush animal back with no contest. When he asks for the set of miniature army trucks, and I shake my head, he calmly carries it up to the cashier and asks if she can keep it for him; then he goes home and forgets about it.

But what about next year? Once he is out there on the playground, at playdates, parties, and school, the stakes will surely go up, and show-and-tell will be about much more than cicada shells in a glass jar.

CHAPTER TWENTY-FIVE

Keeping the Light On

he night air is still on the eve of Nicholas's first day of preschool. A crisp September breeze wafts into our living room through a one-inch crack in the window. The boys are tucked in down the hall. Dave is downstairs rendering architectural drawings and sending e-mails. I am upstairs, half-asleep in an armchair, trying to feel my extremities.

Nicholas's brand-new blue backpack lies against the baseboards by the front door, filled with a required change of clothes that bear his initials in black marker on the washtags.

In thirteen and a half hours, I will strap him and his brother into their car seats and drive one mile to the stone church on the hill, where my firstborn will meet thirteen other people his age and a teacher with whom he will spend three mornings a week.

I'm drunk with giddiness.

Nicholas is excited to be reunited with the red, blue, and yellow articulated earth digger he spotted in the school sandbox on observation day six months ago. I am excited that he is about to make some new friends, feed a goldfish named Lucy, and bring home his first volume of official preschool artwork, which will adorn the fridge and walls. Lest I forget that I am about to have six hours weekly of time alone and with baby Ben.

Choosing a school is an education in itself. There are schools in white clapboard houses and schools in church basements, schools that are free, and others that charge twenty thousand dollars for a year of pre-K; there's Montessori and Waldorf and Sudbury and Reggio Emilia; you have your progressive school, your innovative, your conventional, public, integrated, open, rural, urban schools; schools that work on a reward-and-punishment system, and others that encourage self-realization; schools in which time-outs are against regulations, and others that solve problems in a "magic" circle; schools that require Wechsler IQ testing to get in, and others that take a holistic approach to your child; schools that have a reputation to uphold, that compete state to state, that bell curve up and down; classes of eight children or twenty-five; classrooms with gerbils and turtles, and schools with a caged goat in the backyard.

My friend Jennifer visited a highly reputed school where the director whisked her five-year-old off for forty-five minutes to run a battery of tests. When Jen and her son Max reconvened, the director informed her that her son would not likely be admitted at this time because he couldn't cross his *X* at the midline.

The brochures are like travel guides; the pictures and ad copy tell one story, and the experience tells another—not necessarily better or worse, but different.

It took Dave and me approximately a minute and a half to decide on a school, in large part due to its proximity to our front door. It also had an excellent reputation, and applauded parents for their active involvement. I liked the idea of a co-op system in which a parent could assist the teacher in the classroom during the year. I thought Nicholas would love the blocks, the Lego, the trains and trucks, the Play-Doh and library.

On the first day, Nicholas wears green pants (his favorite color), straps on his backpack, and scurries down the hall toward the classroom where he promptly throws his arms around the neck of the teacher he has never seen before in his life.

In the classroom, he works the crowd like he is at the New Hampshire primaries.

"Hi, Maria! Nice dress you have on. Hi Julie, I like yer long hair. Hi, Emily, dat's a pretty blue shirt wit butterflies. My favorite color is chartroosh. Dat's kind of a lime-ish greenish color, akchally. I like music and trucks. And I have a new baby brother named Benjamin, but we call him Ben-Ben for short."

The mothers leave gradually, blowing kisses, and stroll down the hall to the coffee and cookie table set up in the library for the first day of school. We each take turns sneaking around the corner and leaning an ear toward the door frame of the open classroom where the teacher is narrating a story.

My turn. I hear the teacher asking what is in the picture. I hear my son commenting on the story, wanting to see the tiny picture up close, asking for more detail about a purple bull named Ferdinand. I hear the teacher answering some questions at first; then I hear her telling him to sit down so the others can see, to wait until the end of the story, to sit down again, to be quiet, to sit in a pretzel, to stop talking, to get back to his spot, wait his turn, and sit, sit, sit *down.*

The next day, she gathers fourteen three-year-olds in a circle and sings a song about being quiet.

"Zip those lips," she chants, gesturing at her mouth with her fingers. "Zip, zip, zip!"

Nicholas pantomimes the song with rapt attention. Moments later, she asks the children if it is sunny or rainy. My son shrieks with unbridled enthusiasm, "It's sunny!"

"What season is it?" she continues.

"Fall!" he blurts.

"Let's give someone else a turn," she says.

I instantly recall a magician at a child's birthday party last year who tried to dampen Nicholas's enthusiasm.

"You again?" he quipped when my son volunteered for the third consecutive time after nobody else wanted to do hocus-pocus with Tommy Knucklehead.

Pardon my exuberance.

In the classroom, Nicholas wants to know what lies ahead, who gets to feed the fish, what his role is, what the art project is this morning. He wants to bring his toy lawn mower in for show-and-tell, to see what textures he can make in the classroom Play-Doh with costume jewelry or the wheels of a Tonka truck, to inform the teacher that the maple tree outside the window looks like it has been dipped in cherry juice. He is told to sit down, again, to wait, to zip, zip, zip.

He'll learn to settle down and settle in, I think. This will be good for him. He is going to have to learn to conform to the ways of the world at some point. It's only the first day, for Pete's sake. The teacher is a veteran. She'll know how to handle him.

Ben is asleep. I have two hours to myself on day three of preschool. I fill the kettle and dunk a green tea bag into a large white mug with red letters on its side that read:

STRESS . . .
when your gut says NO
but your mouth says
OF COURSE, I'D BE GLAD TO!

I carry my steeping tea to a well-worn cloth armchair in the living room, where a stack of reading material awaits me on the ottoman. I take my place and exhale. I lean back into the chair, and put my feet up.

Suddenly, something catches my eye on the floor. A Cheerio. I try to ignore it, but it seems to be glaring at me. Winking. Expanding. Multiplying. I try to keep reading. But the Cheerio is heckling me now, hurling epithets in my direction. I will not be cowed. I'll introduce Cheerio to Hoover later. I have now read the same paragraph five times. That's it. I bound forward and snatch the O in my hand. And the piece of hardened green Play-Doh next to it. I fall to my knees and begin speed-cleaning. I crawl across the carpet, gathering toys, balls, stuffed animals, Tinky Winky, magnetic trains, drumsticks, bath dinosaurs, Dipsy and Laa-Laa, colored plastic cups, board books, makeshift magic wands, and farm-animal puzzle pieces. I do the puzzle. Fluff the sofa pillows. Where's Po? I take apart the couch. I find the vacuum attachment I've been looking for to suck sand out of the sliding-door tracks. Where the heck is Po? I organize the vehicles on Nicholas's shelf. Parallel park the dump truck, fire engine, crane, and garbage truck which rattles. Empty bin. Po!

I begin placing books on the shelf next to Nicholas's bed, from largest to smallest. *Rap A Tap Tap, Alison's Zinnia, The Remarkable Farkle McBride, The Children's Book of Virtues, The Little Engine That Could.* "I *think* I can, I *think* I can," I whisper under my breath.

My tea is cold. The microwave hums as I rearrange alphabet magnets on the fridge door. The *P* is missing. So are the *Q,, X,* and *W*. I lie on my stomach on the kitchen floor with a flashlight pointed under the fridge. I retrieve two uncooked spiral noodles, a shriveled grape, the missing *P* and *Q* caked in dusty grease, and eighty-three cents in loose change.

I should sit, sit, sit down. But instead of reading in my chair, sipping antioxidants, stimulating my mind with new ideas, I am slithering like a garden snake on dirty linoleum, finding my *P*'s and *Q*'s and enough money for chewing gum.

Housework is world order.

Ben is awake. It's almost time to pick up Nicholas at the school on the hill.

At the pick-up door, he flies through the crowd yelping, "Mommy! Hi, Mommy! I missed you!" We hug in the entrance, and I can feel his delight. He must have had a great morning. I feel dizzy with love and pride. My baby is out there in the world already, and he's happy. He'll make good friends. He'll *be* a good friend. We'll invite his class and teacher to his birthday party next February. Fill the kitchen walls with his class projects.

The next day, his teacher drops by our house for a scheduled visit, something she does with every student at the beginning of the year.

"Would ya like a delicious chocolate chip cookie? We made them with whole wheat flour and eggs and oil. They're da-licious!" Nicholas says to his teacher.

She declines; then she watches as he proceeds to embark upon his late-afternoon ritual of speaking in tongues while diving behind the couch. Unfamiliar with this behavior, she looks rather bemused.

I expect small talk, pleasantries, a few superficial segues to our inaugural conversation about my son's first school morning. But instead, she turns to me and says, "He has trouble controlling his impulses, doesn't he?"

I glance at my three-and-a-half-year-old, at first to verify that he is in fact still three and a half, then to check his reaction as she discusses him derogatorily in the third person while he stands right next to her. Is he wearing his I-can-hear-even-though-I'm-not-looking-at-you face? Is it the look that means, I heard what you said about me and even though I don't know what the word "impulse" means but do know what the word "trouble" means . . . Am I in trouble?

I motion for the teacher to follow me to his bedroom where I can show her around. Nicholas prances downstairs to play.

Teacher and I stop in front of his bedroom closet, a wall of mirrored sliding doors. We are positioned so that I am talking simultaneously to her face and to her back. She squints at me, her brow knit like she is listening to static and trying to make out an intelligible word.

I tell her that, in fact, Nicholas is the kind of kid who won't touch a brownie on his dinner plate until he has finished the rest of his meal. I'm conscious of not feeling and sounding defensive. I want to give her information so that she can get to know him. I speak calmly to clarify this obvious misunderstanding. Once she knows what makes him tick, I assume, she'll see him in a better light, she'll be happier to have him in her class, and he'll have a good experience as a result.

But it seems we have entered a dense and murky forest. She is disturbed that he painted at the easel for less than a minute, adhered only one happy-face sticker to his placemat art project, and then wandered around the room aimlessly.

I clear my throat as my thoughts scramble for order. It's a throat-clearing that smacks of diplomacy with a touch of restraint. I want to like her. I want her to like my son.

I recall that the classroom's art station offered two paint pots at one time, and I suspected Nicholas might have lingered at an easel with more colors. He's not wild about stickers, and well, wandering is his way of processing a new environment. But I don't want to criticize her curriculum or carefully thought-out room.

I point to the framed paintings on his walls that he did during the summer, in my parents' backyard.

"He calls it rainbow painting," I quip, "because of all the colors he creates by mixing. His favorite color is green."

"I can't get him to sit down during the story," she says with a look of grave concern.

I assure her that he absolutely loves stories, that at twenty months old he wanted Dave and me to open one book and read it to the characters in another book to make a third story. I explain that I understand the need for the children to sit down during her storytelling, and that Nicholas likes to study the picture intently and probably cannot see it well from his spot in the circle.

"Could he sit closer to the book?" I suggest.

She shrugs and mentions that she will make a note of it.

"He doesn't seem interested in any of my projects," she continues. "What *does* he like?"

I recount that from the time he gets up in the morning, he wants to cut planets out of felt, stage puppet shows with flashlights, play water xylophone with glass jars. I mention that he once created a "gravel-making factory" out of funnels, plastic tubing, and paper clips. He wants to wear a hard hat and search the house for stalactites with me, referring to me earnestly as Ms. Frizzle from *The Magic School Bus*. I explain that he is an inventor, that his mind thinks out of the box, and that he is more interested in an object's function than its form.

I'm on a roll.

"He has a lot of energy," the teacher says as she gets up to leave. "My biggest fear is that the other children will reject him. I already see some of them recoiling from him."

I wonder if she is speaking about herself, whether she is foreshadowing her own rejection of him—whether that has already begun after three mornings.

We are deep in the forest now with no yellow ribbons to mark the trail. I am not sure how we got here and feel even less certain of how to get out.

By week two, the teacher is no longer playing "good cop, bad cop" with me. Now she is an aggravated preschool teacher who has no tolerance for any child who can't zip his lips and sit in a pretzel.

I go into preemptive damage control. I pull up a seat in her empty classroom, a tiny wooden chair big enough for Goldilocks. She prefers to stand—over me—arms crossed, while informing me that she has been teaching three-year-olds longer than I've been alive.

"You're being very defensive," she says to me.

I explain that if I sound the least bit defensive, it's because I feel that I must defend my child's right to be treated fairly by her, and that I think she is framing him negatively after so little time and at such a young age, that she hasn't got a clue who he is, and with her negative perception of him won't be inclined to find out, and yes, you better believe that concerns me. I say all this politely, albeit emotionally, using my indoor voice.

"I know you think I don't like your son, but I do," she says, her eyes avoiding mine.

But, she continues to tell me that—after six days—she doesn't know what to do anymore. To underscore her point further, she must let me know that she has no recent memory of ever having to ask a child to sit in a chair and none at all of ever sending a three-year-old out of the classroom.

"I want to be allies," I say to her. "Can we work together for his sake?"

She offers a Mona Lisa smile; then she asks me to come to school with him—and stay.

On my first day of preschool, my three-and-a-half-year-old son is thrilled to introduce me to Lucy the fish. But the fish is not in her tank anymore. Lucy is feeling, shall we say, flushed. I can relate.

I sit in the circle between my son and a little girl who wants to play with my hair. I listen to the story while Nicholas sits transfixed in my lap. I go to music class, shuffle to the library, and file out to the playground. I observe as unobtrusively as I can. Teacher and I catch each other's eye several times. She looks at me in that way that acknowledges that I am observing her observing my son who is observing her observing me.

During playtime, Nicholas wants to do a puppet show with me, and seven classmates join in, the same seven children who follow us to the Lego area to build a ship, the ones who take a ticket stub and board the Rainforest Express where we spot jungle animals out of our imaginary windows. Moments later, the teacher asks me to focus on my *own* child, not the others. I ask what she suggests I do when other children want to join us.

"I don't care *how* you do it, but you need to just focus on Nicholas," she orders.

I feel like I might have a detention coming.

My son and I retreat to a corner where he is inspired to make strawberry ice cream for us by pumping the antennae on the toy telephone. Teacher approaches me after juice and cookies to tell me I'm now doing a "super job."

Over the next few days, I encourage Nicholas to follow the routine on his own while I hang around the school. The director and I become friendly. She describes Nicholas as a creative, loving, free spirit of a child, and I find myself wishing she was his teacher.

This is the real world, I remind myself, the one where a mother can handpick playdates but not teachers. Then a voice inside my head cross-examines the defense. Who is your boy's advocate? Who will speak for him now when he is too young to take the stand?

I poke my head around the door frame to observe my son in the classroom, and suddenly my thoughts flash back eighteen months to a rhythmic crashing sound coming from down the hallway in our house. It sounds as though somebody's trying to break in. I hurry toward the bedroom to find Nicholas standing in his crib with his baby fists wrapped tightly around the railing, hurtling himself back and forth like a baby gorilla. For a second, I think I see a glint of delinquency in his eye. I see trouble. Class clown. Street kid. Jailbird. Baby behind bars. Before I can take my thoughts any further, he yells above the noise, "Mah-mee! I make muzak!" Now, the diabolical glint in his eye is more of a twinkle. Suddenly, the baby gorilla is a brilliant child turning inanimate objects into musical instruments. The mother ready to indict her baby on one count of reckless endangerment with intent to destroy private property now sees him as a budding musician.

A year and a half later, standing in the sanitized halls of my son's preschool, I wonder about how often we misperceive a baby's behavior—and how often we can misunderstand our own children. How does that affect our parenting choices, the way we choose to speak to them, interact with them, discipline them?

A teacher who doesn't like a student is not motivated to get to know him, empathize with him, or engage him.

I want to be my boy's advocate, not make excuses for him.

After several mornings of casual classroom surveillance, I have seen more than I anticipated. A little boy falls down at the front of the front-door lineup and blames Nicholas, who is bundled and waiting at the other end. Teacher takes the boy's word for it. A girl can't find a toy horse for her farm and complains to the teacher that Nicholas, who is playing with a train ten feet away, has stolen it. Teacher suggests the girl ask him where it is.

It isn't rocket science. These children are getting a message from Teacher, who incidentally seemed to have her back turned all three times I witnessed a classmate push, hit, and kick my son without warning or consequence.

"I have fourteen children to watch," she reasons. "I can't notice everything that goes on."

This is enough to make a fly-on-the-wall mom bite her fingernails and pace like an expectant father, but is it the kind of observation that incites a parent to pull a child out of a school and request a refund?

Can a three-year-old come to the classroom with all his parts integrated? What if he doesn't adapt to the environment within the standard six-to eight-week period? What if he does not show the typical signs of adjusting to the routine and his peers by then, of separating from mother like everyone else? Is something inherently wrong?

Doctor G. is a forty-something, affable bearded fellow, with a cluttered desk and an office the size of our walk-in closet. I got his name from a woman who assured me he knew a great deal about very young children and the education system. Maybe he can chart this terrain for us. Maybe he can shine a light on the situation, and reassure us that our son will turn out just fine twenty years from now.

Dave and I arrive for a one-hour consultation. We ask him questions about children and the expectations of teachers, about the dangers of labels, and the potential effects of shame in a little person who is prone to putting his shirt on backward.

"If a preschooler is told to sit down three times a day in September," I ask, "and he finally does so by June, is it because he was told four hundred and sixty-eight times or because he just matured?"

He smiles.

We fill the air with our questions, anxieties, doubt, determination, and devotion. At the end of the session, he concludes that a best-case scenario is that our son has a "not great, but okay" year at preschool. And the worst-case scenario is that this year could turn him off school, teachers, and learning, not to mention himself.

At the door, Doctor G. shakes Dave's hand, then mine, and says something that seems to echo within the four walls of his tiny wood-paneled office.

"You have a long haul ahead of you," he says, nodding at both of us. "The world will try again and again to turn out your son's light. It will be your responsibility to keep his light on, and to teach him how to do the same."

He reminds us that Nicholas is only three, that he doesn't have to be in school right now, that maybe it's not the right time for him, or at the very least, the right teacher. Your decision. Good luck. Keep me posted. That'll be ninety dollars.

The door closes, and Dave and I disappear down the dank stairwell.

I descend into the trenches, talk with other mothers, friends, women at the park and on the Internet, exchanging e-mails with people I will never meet—mothers, school directors, researchers, educators—who lead me to other mothers, school directors, researchers, educators. Word of mouth spreads like pollen in a breeze. I feel energized by the acquisition of new information, the galvanizing power of knowledge.

Janet's daughter Hannah went through a similar experience at her preschool. Because the teacher had singled out the little girl and made an example of her every day, the poor child had nightmares for months on end, stopped smiling, and picked at her food. Janet decided to wait out the year, a choice she now regrets.

I talk with Mindy who couldn't find any school she liked so she started her own. And I bump into Beryl whose son, Darren, is now thriving after she switched schools midyear. Kim took her son, Sam, out of preschool after his baby brother was born so she could spend time with him before he went off to kindergarten, a choice she says proved beneficial for all of them.

I call old friends, cross paths with single mothers, mothers of six, mothers of triplets, mothers of toddlers in programs every day of the week, home-schooling mothers, mothers who enrolled their children in "preschool" when they were eighteen months old, mothers who don't believe children need school before kindergarten, mothers who think it's good preparation, mothers who think children have too much to do, mothers with full-time help, occasional help, no help, and mothers who recommend books—*The Hurried Child* by David Elkind, *The Over-Scheduled Child* by Alvin Rosenfeld, *Magical Child* by Joseph Chilton Pearce, *How Children Learn* by John Holt, *Kids Are Worth It* by Barbara Coloroso, *Raising Your Spirited Child* by Mary Sheedy Kurcinka, *Real Boys* by Dr. William Pollack (Ph.D).

Unlike the grandstanding days of new motherhood, most mothers of school-age children are like colleagues, all part of a collective-bargaining unit working on the same assignment. Mothers I meet now want to help, offer tips, share inside information. Unlike the newborn months when so many of us feel pressured to gloss over our dark fears and ambivalent feelings, the mothers of children who walk out the door every morning are less inclined to sugarcoat. This is bigger than sleeping the night, more important than whose baby is rolling over first or whose cries the least.

I hear voices now, of reason, of purpose; voices speaking the truth; voices that resound with commitment, passion, and conviction. Voices not willing to compromise when it comes to their children's well-being.

We're not comparing children anymore. We're comparing notes. We swap stories.

Rosemary and I sit on a rock near the lake where we live, while her four children play in the sand with my two sons. When her first child, now sixteen, was in kindergarten, the teacher called Corinne her "favorite" and Rosemary and Eric "model parents." But when their third child, Hudson, was in that classroom several years later, the same teacher saw Rosemary and her husband as the little hell-raiser's parents—parents who didn't set boundaries, teach proper socialization skills, issue consequences for unacceptable behavior. Rosemary was now the mother of the kind of child whom she loathed when her daughter Corinne was in preschool. She was now the parent she once judged bitterly.

Rosemary volunteered at her son's school, worked with him at home, in the classroom, on the playground, coached him on how to sit, to play with others, to refrain from grabbing or pushing, to share, to be patient, to understand the needs of others as well as his own.

"I had to be there in the beginning to play go-between, mediator, translator. After a while, when I saw that he *got* it, I took his cue and backed off," she recalls. "As his advocate, I went to the teacher, and I told her that, sure, he's different. I asked her why she was trying to make all the students the same. She didn't want his behavior to change, she wanted the *essence* of Hudson to change. What kind of people were the first explorers? The innovators? The ones who have vision? The world needs more people like Hudson."

She contended with more than his teacher's perception of her son. Rosemary and her husband grappled with the thorny branches of labels.

"He was just Hudson. And he was only four."

Rosemary and her husband decided a label would hold their son back. It wasn't the social stigma of a label that was their concern; it was the internal one, the one that takes form inside a person like a phantom silhouette defining his edges in hard lines. Now, he's a thriving ten-year-old at the top of his class, who still happens to march to the beat of his own drum.

I wonder if Steven Spielberg sat on the circle with his legs in a pretzel when he was four, if he colored in the lines and kept his ideas to himself.

There are people out there—teachers, peers, parents of playmates— who will be good to our children. And there are others who will become our sleepless night. Some will discipline our children harshly in our absence and without remorse or apology. The rare person will go to bat for our sons and daughters. Nobody will love them unconditionally.

Every parent appreciates when a teacher is not the average Joe. Like Mr. Joe, my son's music teacher. He teaches children between the ages of eighteen months and seven. Nicholas is one small face in the crowd. Somehow, in all the activity, Joe has a knack for hearing every voice, for using the language of music to communicate with the shy ones, the boisterous ones, the ones who can't sit still, and the ones who won't move a pinkie no matter how jazzy the nursery rhyme.

He doesn't have the same twenty-five children all week; he has five hundred.

Joe applauds the tone deaf and the ones with perfect pitch. He and his wife Carmen praise effort, not compliance. Joe never halts his class midsentence to reprimand a child for interrupting, squirming, or talking out of turn. He doesn't cast a pall over the room, sending a message to the others that one child is the bad egg. He *could* stop the music. He could say, "I guess we have to wait for little Billy to stop making noise so we can carry on with our class," while the kids sit and stare, their eyes shifting back and forth across the lineup of children.

But that's not his way. There is no shaming in his crowd control. The air is clean. He addresses age-appropriate behaviors—like not waiting for a turn, grabbing, running, yelling—by subtly shifting gears, varying the tone and inflection of his voice in order to make eye contact and collect the students' scattered energies. He does not take a child's overzealousness or lack of participation personally. He doesn't appear annoyed by a student's spontaneity or apparent disinterest.

He simply works harder to reach each child. And it works every time.

On the other hand, there's the arts and crafts teacher who

directed Nicholas and five other children to paint a leaf green and then turn it over and roller it to make a print. After Nicholas had followed this simple instruction, which took about thirty-five seconds, he began to experiment with the roller, creating different patterns and textures. The last thing I remember the teacher saying to me was, "This class is too advanced for him. He was asked to paint a leaf and roller it. And he couldn't do it."

That night, while he's brushing his teeth, I ask Nicholas if he enjoyed the leaf project. He stares at his mirror image, the corners of his mouth still foamy, and says slowly, "I didn't do it right."

I weigh options and odds. If Doctor G. could have guaranteed Dave and me that our son will turn out just fine twenty years down the road, would that have set our hearts and minds at ease?

I don't want the benefit of the doubt. I want the benefit of *no* doubt. But in a world without doubt, what is faith?

What happens to us? Once across the threshold of motherhood, we begin to feel as if the whole thing depends on us, on our good judgment and perfect choices, on how well we mothers can manage and what kind of children we can grow with enough advice, time, and money—like the entire trajectory and outcome of our children's development falls squarely on our shoulders.

Our prayers fall silent. We fall prey, instead, to worry, to relentless anxiety, to anger, to depression. We forget to breathe. We forget ourselves. We forget that our child does not exist to validate or vindicate us, to make us look good or feel better about ourselves. We forget that it's not about us.

We let doubt creep in quietly, stealthily, and we begin our tango with the agony of indecision and the shame of our private fears. Will he be normal? Will she fit in? Will I be wrong? Will he fall between the cracks? Will anybody out there love her? Will I be to blame? Will he love himself? Will he love others? Will she be happy?

To whom do mothers turn when we wonder if we are doing it "right"?

Since my three-and-a-half-year-old is too young to have a discussion about the negative effects of a preschool teacher's rejection—on his desire to go to school, on the dynamics between him and subsequent teachers, on his thirst for learning, and on his perception of himself—I keep my eyes and ears open.

"Mommy," he Nicholas says pensively one afternoon from the backseat of the car. "If you were a mistake . . . you would do everything wrong."

And I knew, like a mother knows anything for sure, that there comes a time, a moment of clarity, when you sense your child's burgeoning selfhood hangs in the balance.

He will have to learn how to sit in the circle, yes. And he will also learn that all living things die, that when you grow up you live in a different house than your parents, that millions of children are hungry, that not all parents love their kids. He will eventually have to conform to the "system," and of course, you can't choose his teachers throughout school. But in that crucial first year, a bad match between teacher and child can lay a faulty foundation for years to come.

Sometimes, you can't tell what's missing until it comes back. And so it was with Nicholas in the weeks after he waved good-bye to the stone school on the hill. We didn't realize how much of his smile had faded until it was restored, until the bounce was back in his step.

How do we teach our children to keep the fire burning inside them in the face of forces that threaten to douse it? Or as a wise kindergarten teacher named Joan once said to me, "A child has an innate need to grow. How can we teach a child to fulfill his needs in such a way that he feels good about himself?"

I want my son to feel he counts, not to feel that he's the *only* one who counts. I want him to sing his own song, but not if it drowns out the songs of others. It is a very fine line. I suppose it's the difference between feeling deserving and feeling entitled.

How can we respect a child's nature, and let it lead at the same time that we encourage it to follow?

CHAPTER TWENTY-SIX

Imaginary Places

wo unthinkable things have happened. First, in some irrevocable turn of events too bizarre to fully comprehend, my four-year-old son has discovered Britney Spears's navel. I thought I was careful. But the boy's powers of observation are devastating.

One minute, my cherub is turning over rocks in search of ants, and the next he is staring hypnotically at a poster of a bejeweled belly button in a store window on our way to buy groceries.

Second, in an absurd departure from logic, Nicholas has tried broccoli. I offered it to him in that foolishly optimistic way mothers offer certain vegetables, and he put the whole floret in his mouth in one swift motion.

Wait, I'm not done yet.

After he swallowed it, he said, "Mmmm! I *love* broccoli!"

Who exactly *is* this small person—and what has he done with my son?

Until this moment, Nicholas's reaction to all things has been borne of that sublime mix of wonder and intrigue. His favorite homegrown game was "The Collection Game," where we roamed the house in search of "intristing things." A broken doorjamb was a stalagmite. Rocks were coins. A hand mirror was a magnifying glass.

A rubber soap dish was a tractor-plow attachment. Just a few months ago, my mother gathered paper clips and wrapped them in masking tape so that he could use them as bales of hay for his miniature farm vehicles.

But overnight, in a neurosynaptic restructuring of his cerebral cortex, he thinks everything is "cool." Dave's banana pancakes are "awesome." The new "sand contraption" he fashions out of straws, rubber bands, and a toothbrush holder is "wicked." Our friend Paul Peress plays drums in an outdoor concert on the shores of the Hudson River, and Nicholas praises him after the show. "Paul, you were great! You were *disgusting!*"

I snuggle him before he leaves for a father-and-son excursion. He wraps his arms around me, and we sway. *One thousand, two thousand, three thousand . . .*

"Okay, that's enough hugging," he declares.

Up until a few months ago, he called me Mommy—"Mahmee"—that cheery, sweet song of a boybird, cooing at dawn, melodic in sunlight, doleful in his hour of need, serenading at dusk. Now, it's a brief and economical "Mom"—unless he's running a fever, has a splinter or a scraped knee, or is startled by the smoke alarm going off when the cookies burn.

"I'm too old to call you Mommy," he explains. "I only call you Mommy if you come back from a trip and I run to you at the airport."

Too old to call me Mommy, but still young enough to stand on the front porch in his Bob the Builder underwear and yell hello to a friend halfway down the block.

"Whatever," he huffs.

"Who talks like that, Nicholas?" I probe.

"Cleo," he says, grinning.

One half hour of *Clifford, the Big Red Dog* while I make lasagna, and shazam, my child is channeling voices.

"It's time for dinner now. Wash your hands, please," I say.

"No way, José," he replies, rather amused with himself.

"Cleo?"

"Max," he corrects, smiling.

"Well, Max, can you tell Cleo, Clifford, yourself, and anyone else you might bump into along the way that they are unfortunately not invited for dinner, that I am looking for Nicholas, my son, and that it's time to eat?"

Six seconds of silence. "Hi, Mom, I'm ba-a-ack!"

"Great to see you, Nicholas! Would you please get washed up for dinner now?"

"Su-ure!"

Between forkfuls of fettucine, he asks, "Mom, what does 'stupid' mean?" The word startles me coming out of his mouth. For a second, I feel like he uttered his first swearword.

"Bobby said it when we were playing trucks," he says, still unsure if it's a greeting or a funny word like "flounder" or "diarrhea."

"Just C-H-A-N-G-E the subject," winks Dave.

"A-N-S-W-E-R it, or pass the Parmesan?" I ask.

Dave and I have entered the famous spelling phase of parenthood. This, so far, has provided first-rate amusement for both of us, as we spell out words and, if necessary, entire sentences that we think might otherwise set the boy's active mind reeling unnecessarily. It also comes in handy for the occasional argument that we vowed we would never have in front of our kids. Try spelling out your disagreements. See how far you get without either misplacing the *e* after *i* or laughing so hard you forget why you were arguing in the first place. Nicholas is at that age where he relishes the sound of his parents giggling, and he joins in while chanting, "Hey, tell *me* the joke, tell *me* the joke!" It occurs to us that someday next week, when he has learned how to spell, we will have to learn Russian.

My friend Leslie's "stupid" story dates back ten years, when her daughter, Alanna, then four, had a friend over. Alanna and Candace were sitting in her bedroom when Leslie walked by and overheard her daughter confiding, "Don't listen to my mommy. She's *stupid*." Leslie froze in the hall.

"I *never* thought that would happen," she says to me. "She and I had this amazing rapport. I felt like it was the beginning of the end. But then I realized that Alanna was out in the world already, trying to assert herself, to have power over me, over her friend. She wanted to be smarter than her mother. I took it personally at first, because at the time I was home with her and thought, well, would she have said that if I was working in an office all day?"

But maybe more revealingly, Candace, who had never known her father, regularly talked back to her mother. Alanna, at the age of four, was trying to identify with her friend, to talk her language—as Leslie put it, "to get into her world."

"Somehow everybody else's approval becomes more important than your own," says Leslie ten years later. "What should we push at home? Our expectations and our disappointment? Then kids grow up feeling they must comply. They don't ask, What are my *own* thoughts? Over the years, the overriding force for my daughter was, Who does the piano teacher, the friend, the group, the soccer coach, the schoolteacher want me to be? And how can I fulfill *their* expectations?"

I want my son to be his own person. But that may be the most complex notion a parent can foster in a child.

Who is he?

Is he who I describe him to be or how he sees himself? Is he an anthology of ancestors inscribed on his blank page? A mosaic of playmates, cartoon characters, and superheroes? Does a mother see her child only through the filter of her own unresolved heart? Or can she see him without bias, and reflect back to him his own self-hood in the making? Will he ever reach a point when he *doesn't* want to be who he is? And where would he go to find a substitute? At the moment, I can think of no greater tragedy.

What is the natural unfolding of a person? Would Nicholas

have been a different person had his brother never existed? Or will he and Ben discover more of themselves through each other?

"Nicky! Hunny!" calls Ben, at eighteen months. "Hunny, come!"

He calls his brother "honey." Within nanoseconds, Nicholas bounces into the room like a human pogo stick, and the two of them begin their high-decibel banter.

"Say hey diddle diddle!"

"Fiddoo."

"The cow jumped over the?"

"Munn!"

"Yeah!"

"Ba-vo!" says Ben, applauding himself.

Rivalry gives way, in rare but encouraging moments, to revelry.

Will the essence of them remain as they grow up? Or will they recreate themselves from borrowed parts that may capture their sensibilities along the way? How can a parent nurture a child's authentic self?

One spring afternoon, Nicholas and I stop by a jazz workshop down the hall from his music lesson. The auditorium is filled with high-school boys and girls who have come to perform rehearsed tunes, jam with professionals, and be critiqued. He sits next to me in the front row, his eyes locked on the stage where the fourteen-year-old drummer organizes his drumsticks in a tool pouch hanging off the snare drum.

Rufus is a towering, sixty-something, upright bass player who stands imposely downstage explaining the dynamics of making ensemble music.

"The most important thing when you are playing with other musicians is to *listen*," he says, cupping his left ear with an open hand.

On his cue, five musicians file up the stairs on the right side of the stage; then they unfold metal chairs and configure them in a semicircle. The theater echoes with the buzz of voices, horns and strings, audience members shuffling in the aisles and stocking video cameras with cassettes. Amid all the commotion, Nicholas gets up and inches his way to the edge of the stage.

"Uh, Rufus?" he calls out somewhat tentatively. I have no clue what he is doing.

"Scuze me, uh, Rufus . . .," he says.

The man turns his head toward the small voice.

"Mm-hmm?" he says, walking right to the edge of the stage, where he stands like the Jolly Green Giant more than six feet above my son's head.

"Um, Rufus?" says Nicholas, his head tilted back forty-five degrees to look up at him. "Uh, you forgot something."

"Oh yeah?" says the Giant.

"Ya hafta feel it in yer *soul*. Yer soul is in *here*," Nicholas says, gently thumping his chest with his right hand.

Rufus grins. He glances over at me, then back at my son.

"You've been here before, haven't you?" he says to Nicholas. "I mean in another life."

Laughter erupts throughout the auditorium.

"Why is everybody laughing?" Nicholas asks me.

"They are laughing *with* you, honey," I say.

"But I'm not laughing," he points out.

I've known this boy now for 1,672 days. I know how brown he likes his toast, how he likes it cut, that he likes his French fries crispy, his milk extra cold, and half a cup of water before bed with three ice cubes. I pretty much know how he'll greet the mailman, what he'll say if the power goes out, when he needs a silent hug, and why he grieves when someone else might shrug. I know what sets him off, lulls him, frightens and comforts him, intrigues, entertains, and baffles him. And yet, on a daily basis, he surprises me. He makes me think ahead of the curve, which requires me to catch the frequent curveball.

"Like I explained before we came down the hill, I cannot carry your tricycle and push you and your brother in the jogger up the hill all at the same time," I say. "You can either leave it here by the tree and we'll get it later, or walk it up yourself slowly."

"I have an idea," he offers. "You can *pull* my tricycle with a rope tow!"

"Nice one, but we don't have a rope."

"Yes, we do!" he pipes, as he yanks the strap from behind the jogger out and lassos it around the bike's handlebars.

Since I'm rather impressed with his ingenuity, I give it a try.

Well, I'll be. Works like a charm.

There is no doubt that there are moments when a mother must stick to her word regardless of her child's battle cry. But if I had stood on that sidewalk and dismissed his idea outright, chastised him about bringing his tricycle in the first place, or walked on without him, it would have been no different than telling him that flexibility, resourcefulness, problem-solving, and teamwork are useless concepts to be altogether avoided.

What messages do we want to convey to a child about his character—and about our own?

Nicholas stands on the arm of the living-room sofa, one foot at the edge, the other swinging back and forth like a Rockette's. He looks as if he's about to jump. Before I can say, "Get dow—," he has propelled himself into the air like a helicopter and landed on the carpet, stunned and amused.

Flipping through a magazine before bed, I spot a blurb about a three-day yoga camp. Not for me, but for Nicholas. Children ages three to five. An hour and a half daily. Maybe a little meditation will be good for him, instill an awareness of mind and body and how the two get along. Maybe instead of just climbing a tree, he can learn to pose like one. Not to mention have some fun in the process.

Nicholas strategizes, "If I like it, I'll stay; if I don't, we can leave. Is that a plan, Mom?"

"That's a plan."

On our drive, Nicholas politely requests the same song on a CD a half dozen times in a row.

"Listen to this, Mom. What's it called?"

"It's called 'Circle Dance.'"

"Listen to 'Circle Dance,' Mom. Are you listening?"

"I'm listening."

In the rearview mirror, I notice that faraway look I've seen in his eyes since he was a baby. He is hanging on a treble clef, notes swirling around his head like hungry seagulls.

"That song sounds like a sunset," he notes.

It reminds me of a time last year when he caught a glimpse of a television commercial in which Big Bird guides a young girl through images of history, from the man on the moon to the Berlin wall coming down. He stood there spellbound, and said afterward, as if in a reverie, "Dat song sounds like a wish is about to come true."

Two minutes after we arrive, Nicholas flashes me a thumbs-up.

"Mom, I like it!" he mouths, smiling.

The class starts, and I take a short walk outside with twenty-eight pounds of baby not the least bit interested in sitting in his stroller and staring at wall shadows. He is so thrilled about everything, doorknobs to dustballs. We stand under an awning to watch and listen to the rain.

"Way-nin," Ben informs me, nodding.

"Yes, it is raining alright," I agree.

I want to preserve his words like an exotic feather, laid carefully between two pieces of wax paper. A "gabboo-gabboo. (garbage truck), "a-na-goo-kam" (another one), "ba-chu-com" (butterfly), "a-changa-cha" (triangle). Gibberish to someone else's ears. A glossary to mine. It's curious how a mother can accept and decipher her child's unique language, yet forget, from time to time, that her child has unique needs too.

After a few minutes, Ben and I enter the building and walk back toward the yoga room to find Nicholas and his teacher sitting in the hallway.

"He is having a hard time listening today," she says patiently, hand on his shoulder. My heart sinks.

"Maybe you can take some time to talk together and join us again. Okay?" she kindly suggests, then slips back into her class.

My four-and-a-half-year-old and I look at each other.

"What's up?" I ask.

"I want *you* to be in the room too, Mom," he says, his voice echoing in the hallway.

"I know you do. But Ben wants to roam the grounds, and your class isn't the right place for that. Sheryl is a wonderful teacher. You are safe here with her. She is kind and fun—plus she knows how to do the lion pose."

I freeze in a silent lion roar, my mouth big as a grapefruit, and Nicholas smiles briefly. I give him the benefit of the doubt and enter the room for a few minutes. The teacher is creatively engaging the kids with magical imagery and songs. Seated against the gym wall are a group of parents whom I would gladly join were it not for my nineteen-month-old playing with the ropes that the assistant is carefully placing on the floor in parallel lines for a game. Nicholas, a pushover for slapstick, cannot imagine anything funnier at the moment than the boy across from him who is rolling himself up in his yoga mat like a hot dog in a bun. Hot Dog begins to giggle, which brings out the unrelenting Cookie Monster in Nicholas.

On the other side of the room, I scoop my baby up with my left arm and briskly walk twenty paces toward Cookie to slip my feet back into sandals. I kneel down, and whisper sternly in my son's ear, "If you don't want to be here, then we can go home and let the other kids have their class. If you want to be here, you need to stay on your mat and listen to Sheryl. What is your decision?"

"I want to stay," he states without hesitation, sitting on his calves in the middle of his mat.

"Good. Have a great class. I'll be in the playground out back."

I close the door, my heart pounding, Ben writhing, parents staring, the other six children looking like smooth marble statues I once saw at the Louvre.

The rain has stopped. I sit on a plastic bag on the wet wooden bench as Ben inspects a toy gas-station pump and car in the private, fenced-in playground conveniently attached to the building. Nicholas is in my mind's eye. I see him in that dim, mellow room that smells like lavender candles. He sits on his green mat, between Ashley on the blue mat and Nicole on the pink mat, my son the jumping bean in the middle of two girls sitting so still I can't say that I ever noticed them blink. Then I remind myself that he has never been Ashley, not even in utero.

He was doing Rimsky-Korsakov's "Flight of the Bumblebee" in my womb, whereas Ben did tai chi. As babies, Nicholas clung to me, and Ben wanted to run free. Nicholas cries despondently over a hangnail, while Ben does a front somersault into the wall, gets up, and carries on. It's a challenge not to compare, not to think of one as being easier than the other.

In fact, if I allow Nicholas's behavior and way of relating to the world to guide me, I can see that if we take his mental and physical energy, add a little separation anxiety and maybe a dash of sibling jealousy to the mix, we have a boy who can't sit on his mat and breathe like a bunny.

Ben is trying to defy gravity and walk up the pink ladder outside Nicholas's class. After a while, we enter the building just as Sheryl walks out of the room, alone. I think, *Here we go. Now she wants to tell me that Nicholas did a back flip off Brad's head and landed in Ashley's lap, that we really ought to go now, that they would waive our fee if they could but sorry they can't.*

"Any better?" I ask, expecting her to read us our Miranda rights.

"Much better," she says smiling. My heart rate slows down.

"I know this may sound odd, but he really does want to be here," I offer.

"I know," she says.

Come again?

"He's a very unique and interesting child," she says, leaning against the door frame. "He's extremely smart. I can tell he has a lot going on in his mind, and that alone must be a lot for him to deal with. It must feel overwhelming."

I realize my mouth is open.

"He has a lot to accomplish in his life," she says, nodding. "And he *will* accomplish it. Once he understands what I'm trying to do in my class, the patterns of group settings, how I teach, what I do with the kids, he will go along with it and be fine."

"That's very insightful of you," I say.

"I have taught children for a long time. And I can't tell you how many out there are just like Nicholas. Children are exactly who and where they are supposed to be at the moment. Nicholas is who *he* is, full of passion and creativity and purpose. And I can see he has the desire to please."

"I want to nurture who he is *and* I want him to sit quietly and follow the class," I say, suddenly feeling as if maybe she understands my purpose too.

"You have to find out *how* he learns—because he does have a way of learning that works very well for him—and then sit down with his teacher at school and tell her so that she will know," Sheryl says.

Nicholas stays in the yoga class and enjoys himself so much he can't wait to come back the next day. Sheryl and the kids slither across the gym floor in the snake pose, stretch their bodies and their imaginations. She leads the group through a lilting chant in Sanskrit.

"Sat-e nam sat-e nam sat-e nam gee . . ."

Sat nam.

Direct translation: true identity.

Nicholas sings along, sits in the circle, legs in a pretzel on his green rubber mat, eyes fixed on Sheryl's face. He had entered that room yesterday with trepidation and unbridled curiosity, which made him squirm, roll, giggle, sing, tickle people and himself, play drum rhythms on the floor with his elbows and heels, and talk incessantly. Because the teacher didn't shame him or shut him out with a chilly *"Now,* where were we?" or ignore him outright, he began to trust her to accept him. To care for him in my absence.

"I am so glad you decided to be here with us, Nicholas!" she said when he returned to the class without me. Music to his ears.

On the way home, Ben, who is not at all pleased about being strapped in a car seat these days, begins to cry. Nicholas covers his ears and wails for him to stop. I try a music cassette. A made-up song. Goldfish crackers. A sippy cup. Nicholas enthusiastically points out an excavator on the side of the road. A flag. A yellow school bus. Nothing works.

Suddenly, the baby whimpers, "A widdo! A widdo!"

"You want a riddle?" I ask, stunned by the timing of his request.

"Yah," he sniffles, catching his breath.

"Okay. What animal looks like a horse but has black-and-white stripes?"

"A zebra!" yells Nicholas.

"What sound does a horsie make?" I ask.

"Neeeee-hee-hee-hee," answers Ben.

I see that, even as a young toddler, Ben has a way of learning, too. Of thinking. Of coping with his own temporary frustration and discomfort. He hasn't thus far put a verb and a noun together, yet he can tell me what motivates him—what drives him.

Under the glow-in-the-dark stars stuck to Nicholas's bedroom ceiling, we say our prayers.

"Goodnight, Nicholas. I love you," I say looking in his blue-turned-hazel eyes reflecting the light from the table lamp next to his bed.

"I love you too, Mom. And you're sorry for raising your voice at me today," he says, holding my cheeks in his warm palms.

He pauses.

"And I'm sorry for getting a little crazy today," he adds.

"We all get a little crazy sometimes," I say.

I am compelled to redefine my rules of conduct, to ponder how brilliance and chaos can begin to resemble one another. I am also compelled to *believe*. If there is one person out there who will see a child in a positive light when others might not, then there must be others.

Three months later, I sign Nicholas up for a trial art class, because he thinks he's "no good at art." My son lasts about thirty-five minutes before he begins his vaudeville number with the blue plastic chair he doesn't want to sit in anymore. Later, when I call Gina, the teacher, to let her know if we'll return the next week, she spends a good forty minutes asking about my child. What I defensively expect is her diplomatic indictment of him, of me, but what I hear instead is her interest, her desire to know my boy and find a way to him.

"I'm in it for the long haul," she chuckles. "I'll do whatever you want. I could work with him one-on-one for a couple of weeks if you like, as well as in the group class, and take it from there. You tell me."

I park in front of the brown brick building to pick up Nicholas after his first class, and stand outside the big window. There, standing at the back-wall board next to Gina is my four-and-a-half-year-old son, black marker in hand, writing eight giant, jiggly, gorgeous letters. I watch through the glass as the two of them exchange muted high fives. He is writing his own name, something he has never done at home despite our most creative cheerleading. Gina drew green dots (his favorite color) as joining points, and he connected them.

"Hello-o-o?" I chime.

"Mom! Close your eyes! Close your eyes!" he screams, and guides me to the back wall.

"Okay. Open them! Ta-da! Look! I wrote my name! I did it! I wrote my own name! Nicholas! That's me!"

When he hugs Gina at the door, she gets down on a knee and says, "We're going to do great work together, Nicholas. You're a treasure."

My heart feels so big at the moment, I want to donate all my worldly possessions and make split-pea soup for the entire neighborhood.

There are those defining moments when you know an identity is in the process of becoming. As parents, we discover where our children thrive and where they falter, how they learn, how they react when they fail, and why. Does he give up? Does he jump right in or need to observe from the sidelines first? Is she a self-starter, or does she need a lot of prodding? Is she a leader, a follower, a team player, or an iconoclast? Is he rocking the boat, questioning the way the world works—or the way one teacher does? Does he want to do it his way because he doesn't want to take direction—or because he has a better way?

Sometimes we gather our best information in the most unlikely circumstances. I recall a conversation Nicholas and I had about Halloween costumes while driving home one afternoon from the grocery store. He was two and a half years old.

"Do you want to be a lion?" I asked.

"No fenks."

"How about a firefighter?"

"No."

"Do you want to be a marching-band drummer?"

"No."

"We could make you a tall hat with a green feather and a drum that you can wear," I offered.

"No fenks."

"So, what do you want to be?" I ask.

"A mountain," he answered, staring out the window.

"Okay. Uh, how would we make that costume?"

"A quarter note," he changed his mind.

"You want to be a quarter note?" I echoed.

"No," he hedged.

"How about a construction worker, or an architect like Daddy? You could wear his hard hat."

"No, no," he decided. "I juss wanna be myself."

He went out for Halloween dressed in green corduroys and an orange turtleneck, the same clothes he had worn all day. When people asked him what he was, he shrugged and said, "Me."

How many seemingly inconsequential interactions do we have with our children in which their unspoken message is clear: *I want and need to be myself.* Or more poignantly, *I want to be accepted for who I am.*

And how often can we hear ourselves inadvertently implying: *You can be yourself as long as it's who we and everyone else want you to be.*

We don't always communicate the disparities in words. Sometimes, we coax a child to swim upstream, making him work against his own current. Somehow, we can resist a child's natural inclination, parenting *against* his need and nature. Push one child and he forges ahead, but push another child and she withdraws. How do we parent so that a child's nature does not turn against himself? How can we parent each child according to who he is, tailoring our approach and attitude to embrace his unique sensibilities—respecting his soft spots as well as his strong points?

And how many children might turn inward because they feel their own little world is preferable to the big one out there—or turn outward to deflect the pain of being in their own skin?

What is a child's own individual nature, and what does that nature have to do with his learning—and our parenting?

"I think we are born with a poker hand," says my longtime friend and mother of four, Rosemary. "And that personality is then either okay with the world or the pressure is on to change it. Make him quieter. More extroverted. Give him a sense of humor. A stronger will. A father may put his son in every aggressive sport in order to make him tougher, turning him into a ball of anger, and the affectionate sweet little toddler grows up to become a powder keg. Or a mother may hush her small daughter every time she whines about something someone said or did to her, urging her instead to smile and go along with things; then she becomes an adult who can't speak up for herself, a doormat, a victim. Even a well-meaning parent can break a child's spirit."

We want to give our children the room to have their own characters even as we try to teach them how—who—to be. Be polite. Be cooperative. Be quiet. Speak up. Be generous, but don't give too much. Have a mind of your own, but be obedient. Be an individual, but blend in. Express yourself, but don't rock the boat. Tell the truth, unless it's not what people want to hear. Don't compare yourself to others, but don't live in a bubble.

Who are we afraid our children will become if we stop trying to define, even alter, their characters? Do we think they will be better people if they reflect back to us our own ideals? Sometimes we let our fantasies obstruct our ability to parent in the warm light of acceptance. Isn't it then possible that we unwittingly give our children the sense that we wish they were more like someone else, less like who they are?

If we can stay tuned to our children, and get to know them as they grow and change, allowing *them* to teach *us* who they are, then we may sense when they might be at risk of losing their way.

If I want my children to lay claims on their true identities—their *sat nam*—and grow into their own shoes, I have to do the same. And if I think I've learned anything in the last few years, it is no doubt a small star in a constellation that lies ahead. Thinking of imaginary places yet uncharted, I simultaneously draw blanks and paint elaborate portraits of the future. My friend Gale told me that, in many ways, her children's adolescence reminds her of those first few years from birth to five, the dance of dependency and autonomy, of holding on and letting go. When you look at it from that vantage point, these journeys of ours seem more like cycles of life than straight lines.

Parenthood is savory humble pie, baked fresh daily.

"Make a wish, Mom," says Nicholas, the two of us standing in front of a fountain at the mall.

"Hmmm . . . I wish for Nicholas and Ben to always be happy," I say dreamily as I toss a rusty penny into the water.

"Well, sometimes I'm happy, and sometimes I'm sad," he reasons.

"That's true. Well, then I wish for you to always know how much I love you." I resume my reverie, and plop another cent into the well.

"But I already know that," he retorts.

"Okay. You make a wish, then," I say, handing him a nickel.

"This is worth a big wish," he declares, and with his hand in the air, says calmly, "I wish . . . for Ben to stop screaming."

The silver coin settles underwater on a dark blue tile, and I try to wring my mind dry of imaginary places that bear no resemblance to reality.

"Can you make it less dark, please?" Nicholas whispers from his bed. I flick on the hall light and hear him rustle in his crisp sheets.

I press my lips to his forehead, close my eyes, and remember the words of Doctor G. who spoke with Dave and me one night last year about bright lights and dark roads. *The world will try again and again to turn out your son's light. It will be your responsibility to keep his light on, and to teach him how to do the same.*

I am just beginning to understand that in order to truly trust in our children and ourselves, we have to keep our own light on. This isn't simply about having the courage to stand up for what we believe in, but having the courage to doubt, to change, to *be* changed.

After the boys are asleep, I gaze at my dandelion bouquet wilting in a small glass on the kitchen counter, a gift from Nicholas. And I think, Somewhere, there's a place for him.

On a good day, I can clearly imagine that place. On a day when I lack the convictions of my courage, I sit slouched behind the wheel at a red light and read the bumper sticker on the car in front me that says, PRAY. And then I see another sticker on a delivery truck passing me on the right: IT'S TOO LATE TO TURN BACK.

And, in some eerie moment of synchronicity that I may never forget, I catch a glimpse of a sticker on the silver fender of an old white Cadillac pulling out of a gas station that reads, LUCKI LU.

That throws a bucket of cold water on the embers of my fears. For a while anyway.

Somewhere in the world, there *is* a place for Nicholas. For Ben. For children everywhere. They will each bring the world home with them a little at a time, and they will bring a lot of themselves to the world, and with any luck, it'll be a better place because of them.

I spend a few minutes dithering around my desk, sorting through dusty stacks of books and file folders, when I unearth a piece of paper bookmarked inside a volume of poems by Rainer Maria Rilke I had been browsing through several years ago—before I became a mother.

As I read the typewritten words, I realize that the letter in my hand was written to a baby girl or boy I had not yet met.

One week to go, my little one . . .
One week to our first glimpse of your sweet face.
One week to go before we hold your tiny palms, study
    your fingers, nuzzle the creases in your neck.
Seven days until we finally meet.
I will no longer wake up the same way.
I will be your mother.
Will I look different in the mirror?
Will I see the world through new eyes?
How will I be changed by you, my little one?
Who will you be?
And . . . who will I become because of you?

My letter to Nicholas had been sleeping inside a book all these years, laying dormant on a dog-eared page, keeping the place of a poem I liked that asks me to be patient with all the questions in my heart, because, in some distant day, I will live my way into the answers.

ACKNOWLEDGMENTS

'm sitting in a postpartum funk one afternoon five years ago—eight weeks after I had given birth—when the mail arrived. In the pile was a letter from a literary agent in New York who had read a piece I had written for *The New York Times*.

"Do you have any ideas for a book?" she wondered.

And here we are. Meredith Phelan, *thank you* for minding my p's and q's with such zeal over the years, for reading on trains, planes, and subways because it couldn't wait until later, for your whole-hearted faith in me and this book. Every writer should be so lucky.

Halfway through this journey, Meredith joined Judith Ehrlich Literary Management. And so to you, Judith Ehrlich, I extend my heartfelt thanks for your stalwart support, your canny ability to see the forest *and* the trees, and for paving the yellow brick road to the Flatiron Building.

I am wildly grateful to St. Martin's Press. It was my divine fate to work with editor Jennifer Weis, who makes mothering four children and publishing books look like pie, and whose brilliant instincts and genial spirit made this a hugely memorable ride for me. Thank you, Jennifer! I offer tremendous thanks to impeccable assistant editor

Stefanie Lindskog, publicity dynamos John Murphy, John Karle, Carrie Hamilton-Jones, marketing wizards Matthew Baldacci and Dori Weintraub, dogged serial rights manager Caroline Sparrow, clever cover designer Sarah Delson, and book designer Gretchen Achilles for your dedication and enthusiasm.

Thank you to Discovery Health Channel's Donald Thoms and Marly Carpenter. And to Shannon Martin and Samantha Allen, for going the extra mile.

To my good pals at North South Productions: Charlie De-BeVoise, Wendy Woll, and all my colleagues who *Make Room for Baby*, thanks for your support and friendship.

To my friends and colleagues at *Fit Pregnancy*, Carole Lucia, Peg Moline and your tireless staff, thanks for your support of my writing over the years. I'm proud to write for a magazine that inspires expectant and new mothers to feel and be their best.

A special tip of my hat to Kathleen Whitfield and Nancy Jo Bykowski of *New Beginnings* magazine and La Leche League International, and to co-founder Marian Tompson, for your graciousness, time and commitment.

Blessings to my true blue pal Debbie Robinson for taking the detours with me.

Special quarter-century thanks to Lori Meed for believing. Abiding thanks to all those friends who took the time to read—Deborah Groper, Rosemary Danielis, Jennifer Lisimachio, Jennifer Jonas, Maria Danilowicz, Jeff Sykes, Marianne Salama, and Elona Picker. Bear hugs to Leslie Taylor-Houston and all those mothers who shared stories with me.

My deep appreciation to E. Jean Carroll, Mark Victor Hansen, Dr. William Sears, June Cotner, Julie Moran, Jane Gabbert, Dr. Jack Newman, Tine Thevenin, Ann Anderson, and Dr. Jane Greer.

Thanks to my friend Kevin Buckley, for sitting at The Bay Leaf restaurant with me and suggesting that *Let the Baby Drive* be the title of the book, not just a chapter in it.

To Ken Lindner & Associates, especially to Kristin Allen, mom, friend, and television agent, who always had a hunch.

I owe eternal thanks to my husband, David, for making banana pancakes from scratch every Saturday morning, for prodding me to forge ahead when I had no idea where I was going, for fathering our boys with such heart and creative spirit. Isn't this fun?

A world of gratitude to my parents for letting your baby drive. To "Agapi," for pulling wild daisies by the side of the road after my piano lessons, for interrogating my boyfriends, and raising me to believe that I could do anything. And to "Grampi," for moving mountains, for your grace under pressure, and for Tupperware dinners during rehearsals. Nobody could have loved or given me more.

To "Auntie Noo Noo," from the moment you set eyes on Nicholas and Ben, you have loved them like they were your own. Thank you for knowing the way to a child's imagination, and for offering so much of yourself, your time, and your heart to us.

To "Unko Greg," who teaches with a gentle spirit, you have a way of knowing exactly what a person needs and when they need it. (Thanks for fixing the rear bannister.)

To my perenially supportive in-laws, Joan and Don, thanks for always being there for our family.

And of course . . .

To Nicholas, my firstborn, for driving lessons: I never kept a fancy photo album for you with a lock of your hair in a blue ribbon or your weight stats neatly written in calligraphy month by month. (We did, however, keep a pee, poop, nurse, and nap journal of your first six months, which you are more than welcome to flip through at your leisure someday.) I humbly offer you this book instead, and hope that when you read it, you will remember where you started, feel proud of where and who you are, and know how much I have always loved you.

And to Benjamin, my second firstborn: you love jokes and corn on the cob and wearing hats and drop-in company. Even at the crack of dawn, your eyes dance with the light of a thousand stars. As time passes, the lessons you teach me will fill many pages to come. I love you, my dear Ben-Ben. "Why da sock kwoss da woad? Da chicken's coming! I ged it!"

Finally, ultimately, I thank God for the gift of motherhood, for divine inspiration, for filling my heart with questions, and reminding me always of why I am here.

Printed in the United States
142976LV00001B/6/A